Christmas 1991

To Arne
    From Don

PISTE AGAIN
A GUIDE TO SURVIVAL SKIING
Barry Waters

Queen Anne Press
Macdonald and Co
London and Sydney

For Lizzie

A QUEEN ANNE PRESS BOOK
© Barry Waters 1982

First published in hardcover in 1982 by Queen Anne Press,
a division of Macdonald & Co (Publishers) Ltd,
Maxwell House, 74 Worship Street, London EC2A 2EN
A BPCC plc Company

This edition first published in 1984

Illustrations by Graham Thompson

British Library Cataloguing in Publication Data:
Waters, Barry
   Piste again.
   1. Skis and skiing — Anecdotes, facetiae,
satire, etc.
   I. Title
   796.93'0207   GV854.3

ISBN 0-356-10537-7

Reproduced, printed and bound in Great Britain by
Hazell Watson & Viney Limited,
Member of the BPCC Group,
Aylesbury, Bucks

Contents

Introduction

'May I take this opportunity of thanking all of those who
went skiing last year while drawing dole money and social
security. This not only proved my long stated opinion that
it's cheaper to go skiing than to stop at home, but also
helps me to persuade the hoteliers to share my optimistic
view of Britain's sound economic future . . .'

Letter from a West Midlands travel agent to his clients in 1981

There was a time when the Alps were the preserve of mountain folk, convalescents, British milords and a few eccentric members of the upper classes who went in for something called ski-running.

Times have changed. Ski-running has turned into skiing and the sport has long since lived down its exclusive origins. The Alps in winter have become the Central Park of Europe and the Abominable Townsman is there in force, making his strange tracks across the snow, pimpling the slopes with his moguls and finding all the satisfactions of the rat race on the overcrowded *pistes* and lifts.

For most of us there is now no escape. Far from being something few can afford, there are few today who can afford *not* to put in an annual appearance on the slopes. A winter holiday is as obligatory as a summer one, the snow tan as socially necessary as the beach tan, and parallel skiing as vital a skill as driving a car.

Normally sensible people have now come to regard it as perfectly natural to spend at least two weeks a year on the high ground, wearing a fortune in gaudy, uncomfortable clothing, risking broken limbs and cracked ribs, exposing themselves to frostbite, frozen lung and snow-blindness, and being advised by the sons of local crofters how best to slide down hills with boards strapped to their feet.

Even devout cowards can be seen hurtling downhill at close to terminal velocity, icicles up their nostrils, snowflakes attacking their eyeballs, and then voluntarily repeating the experience.

Skiing is now permanently established in the middle classes' conversational Top Ten and it may not be long before most of us have a plug-in miniature mogul slope in the back bedroom so that we can practise rolling our knees in the off-season. They have even fitted up glaciers for year-round sliding for people who miss their two winter weeks or can't bear to hang up their boots for the summer.

Surprisingly, perhaps, there has not so far been much organised resistance to all this. Few people complain openly about their annual ordeal on the slopes and some even profess to derive a bizarre pleasure from it. Suggestions that there are more enjoyable ways of stretching your legs in the mountains seem to have gone unheard.

So it looks as if we may have to learn to live with this new burden in our lives, condemned to spending two weeks a year on the snow and the other fifty talking about it – a penance we pay for comparative prosperity.

But things are not as bad as they sound. Techniques for getting by on the slopes have evolved rapidly in recent years and the reluctant *piste* basher need despair no longer. He or she may never be able to ski, but that is no reason not to succeed on the slopes. The art of Survival Skiing, as it's known, has transformed the sport for the millions who have discovered that there are plenty of ways of getting to the top of a mountain and down again with a minimum of effort and a maximum of kudos. Winter holidays are no longer a pleasure reserved for *piste* beasts and people who don't like having things easy. The Survival Skier can keep his end up with the best of them and, indeed, probably finds more challenges and enjoyment in his version of the sport than the Real Skiers do in theirs.

This book is intended as a guide to some of the basic Survival Skiing techniques, unorthodox in some cases, but effective none the less, and decidedly less strenuous than more conventional ways of skiing. It is written in the belief that most skiers, deep down, or perhaps not so deep down, are not that young any more, don't like heights or snow, would be upset if they broke a leg and just want to get through the day with a flush on their cheeks, a few tales to tell and their skiing ego intact.

1. Skiing and Being Seen

**'Parallel skiing . . . I indulge in now only as I stop in front
of a restaurant.'**

Irwin Shaw

Anyone who has been to a ski resort will know that there is a lot more to skiing than merely sliding about on snow. It is not just a nifty way of travelling from A to B in winter. For one thing, when done with an all too common panache, it's an extremely flamboyant method of getting around.

It does not take long to dawn on most beginners that the chap who has just swished down the slope to a snow-spraying deadstop in front of the restaurant terrace, pushing his glasses on top of his head, need not have done so in quite such a distastefully showy fashion.

Nevertheless, it must be admitted that to some people this is what skiing is all about. The so-called 'Look, Ma' mogulfields in front of the restaurant or under the chairlifts at some American resorts were not idly named. Many people ski simply to be seen. And we may as well concede that most of us aspire to ski in a way that would be worth being seen. To judge by the average skiing conversation, of course, most of us already do.

Survival Skiers soon learn, however, that discretion is the better part of exposure on the ski slopes and that it is not wise to try to beat the exhibitionists at their own game. This does not necessarily mean, though, that you have to defer to the showmen just because they can ski better than you. The point is that you don't really need to ski like that in order to feel that you can ski like that.

The secret of it all is that 'skiing is believing'. And to make belief in yourself as a skiing ace possible there is a universally accepted code among Survival Skiers

---

Rules of Skiing

SELF-KNOWLEDGE

No-one skis like he thinks he skis.

Most 'parallel skiers' can't.

The best skiers talk the least.

Anyone who says he knows how to ski probably can't.

Anyone who says he gets by is probably very good.

Every skier has some advice for every other skier.

If you try to show someone a thing or two, you will be shown up.

which, put simply, amounts to: 'You believe in me and I'll believe in you'. So, provided you feel the part, and most do (the gear is a great help in this make-believe), and provided you get the ego-boosting support of your comrades in adversity, there is no reason to let lack of ability cramp your style.

The Survival Skier is much helped in all this by that fundamental principle which applies to most sports — if not most human activities — that more enjoyment is derived from talking about it than from actually doing it. It is easy to be misled into thinking that skiing is an action-packed participatory sport. And, for obvious reasons, enthusiasts try to put this around. But don't be deceived.

The confusion arises because skiing provides a thousand opportunities for talking about it while seeming to be doing it. This may indeed be the secret of the success of skiing. Most of the time is spent standing in queues or admiring the view or listening to the instructor or taking refreshment. Yet everyone involved in these activities claims to be 'out skiing'.

However, although this apparent active participation is, in fact, essentially passive, there will be certain Moments of Truth. The Survival Skier's aim must be to keep these to an absolute minimum. Your first step should be to plan your holiday very carefully, bearing in mind that the Survival Skier's success or failure is often determined well before he reaches the ski-station.

Don't make the mistake of trying to limber up for the slopes by going to the local dry ski-school. This will only undermine your confidence, and to the Survival Skier, confidence is all. Besides, that plastic matting is jolly hard and it hurts when you fall. Instead, devote your time to selecting the right kind of resort.

The best bet is still the traditional type of ski village — not the purpose-built ski-straight-from-your-balcony resort. The reason for this is that you need to spend as much time as possible actually getting out to the slopes. The old style of village is more likely to ensure this and to provide plenty of plausible reasons for delays *en route*. The modern resort with its ubiquitous conveyor belts and buggy carts and snow-mobiles and mini-trains and lifts of all types to transport you around (why walk anywhere when you can waste a little more of the world's energy resources?) provides far fewer excuses.

You should also check the snow reports over a period of several months. Look for resorts with consistently bad weather. The worst possible conditions for the Survival Skier are bright sunshine, perfect visibility, no wind and excellent snow.

If you pick a sufficiently low-lying station, you may even be lucky enough to find there is no snow at all, or at least, not enough to ski. If you go much below 1,000 metres, though, people may begin to wonder if you ever wanted to ski in the first place. Be careful, however, that this doesn't backfire on you. A shortage of snow can mean all the skiers being concentrated in one area in full view of one another. This is fatal for the Survival Skier who generally wants as much space,

as much tree cover, and as many mountain hideaways as possible.

So study the *piste* maps in the brochures carefully. The Survival Skier will want good access to other neighbouring skiing areas, with plenty of scope for darting from bar to bar and lots of interconnecting routes, ideally via sheltered woodland trails. Above all, try to find somewhere with as many ways down as possible. Finally, always try to pick a resort where the standard of skiing is likely to be low.

2. Gear

'Do you sell ski-wear?'
'Yes. But not really the kind you can ski in'
Overheard in mountain ski boutique

The main thing to think about before you go is gear — no minor matter and, for many, one of overriding importance. Indeed, to some skiers, equipment is all. Even when you've got to the resort gear is likely to occupy rather more of your time than skiing. For if one tenth of your holiday is spent skiing, you can be sure that at least three tenths of your time will be spent dressing and undressing, fiddling with your equipment, discussing it and, of course, shopping for more gear.

The latter is one of the principal *après-ski* rituals, usually taking place between 4.30 and 8.00 pm, thus getting the evening off to an expensive start and giving you something to talk about during dinner. Basically, the aim is to duplicate items you already have on the pretext that the new acquisition has some indispensable additional refinement. Thus you end up with a hat featuring an even louder motif, goggles fitted with windscreen wipers or boots with temperature controls.

Many of these articles, in turn, will be quietly discarded at the end of the year so that the whole cycle can begin again next season. In the ski game disposability is all, and few industries can boast a better trained set of throwaway consumers.

You will gather from this that ski-wear is closely related to fashion — and often

to be found leading the way rather than following. Whereas once town togs were adapted for the mountains, ski-wear now sets the trend in the towns. Do you know anyone who does not wear an anorak for Saturday morning shopping? A ski manual published not so long ago advised skiers to 'travel out wearing a lounge suit, overcoat, gloves and scarf which may all be used for evening wear'. Do you know anyone now who would dare to dress like that in a ski resort?

We are not just talking here about High Street fashion. Ski-gear is *haute couture* as well. There is almost certainly more interest in which is 'the ski' this winter, whether ski lengths are up or down, and whether the new boots are rear entry or side entry than in what Dior or Cardin are doing with hemlines.

In fact, it's very hard work keeping up with the fashion, flitting as it does from striped boiler suits to puffy jackets, from sleeveless overvests to sweaters or from baggy pants back to the traditional *Keilhosen*.

One of the sport's many agonies is deciding which items in your ski wardrobe to pack. Will the jockey look still be in? Will you look out of place this year in your balloon silk windshirt and your pants with the gathered ankles? Should you take your gaiters with you this time — and if so, the plain or the striped, and which way striped? Those damned 'go faster' stripes will keep changing direction, depending on whether it's broad chests or long legs that are in.

Colours complicate things even more. At one time blue on the slopes was as standard as the black of Henry Ford's Model Ts. Now everyone's in technicolour, doing their best to keep up with the shade of the month.

The purpose of all this pantomime, of course, is to take the average skier out

---

Rules of Skiing

CLOTHING

Every skier wears at least five different colours.

One of your zippers will jam often.

You are constantly in search of some new item of clothing or equipment.

Anyone with top-of-the-range gear is probably not a top-of-the-range skier.

Any gear you buy in the resort can always be found cheaper at the pre-season or after-season sale in your local ski shop at home.

All glasses and goggles are guaranteed to mist up in bad weather.

You will rip, stain or lose an item of clothing every few days. It is most likely to be your most recent purchase.

of himself, to encourage him in his delusion that on skis he really is a different person, and a bit of a hotshot at that. Most Survival Skiers go along with this approach and take advantage of the props available. It is, after all, easier to swap technical talk if you are the possessor of items like a skin-tight suit, a pointed helmet, mono-ski wings under your arms and skis which let the air through the aerodynamic holes in the tips.

The Old-Timer

But there are exceptions. One is the Survival Skier who achieves excellent results by dressing 'down' rather than 'up' for skiing. He clings resolutely to his old lace-up leather boots, Telemark era skis and cable bindings. His outfits also are suitably dated – knickerbockers and knee-socks are a great favourite. The colours he chooses are neutral and well faded; pale blues or khakis are the most popular as they are easy to get lost in and have a vaguely military flavour – perfect for muttering about high mountain training in Norway after the war.

Anyone who decides on this sort of outfit must be prepared to see the part through. The aim is to come over as the self-reliant loner who has seen a lot of snow. These types of Survival Skier are usually irrepressibly cheerful and distinctly unimpressed by the latest ski technology. ('I'm a bit of an old ski-tourer, myself . . . How do you get on with those new plastic boots? Not much to chew on if you get buried somewhere. Do you think they're here to stay?')

Another favourite prop is a sealskin strip, tucked in the belt, for ski-walking uphill. ('Never know when you may need it . . . don't trust these lifts much.') Their only colourful indulgences are a multi-coloured set of waxes and a bloodstained kerchief, once used as a tourniquet and kept as a souvenir.

Old-Timers also specialise in interesting homemade refinements to their equipment – every bit as good a talking point as the latest in fuel-injected skis. Some, for instance, do without ski-stoppers or *lanières*. ('Anyone silly enough to lose a ski deserves to walk.') Others remove the straps from their sticks. ('Never again – not since I failed to slip them in an avalanche in the old days and broke both my wrists.')

Skilful use of the bum-bag is another stock-in-trade. Theirs usually contain a fascinating jumble of bits and pieces which they lose no opportunity to tip out and display. Standard items include maps, compass, avalanche cord, crêpe bandages, spare ski-tip, splint, whistle, various kinds of twine, klister, assorted clips, Factor 15 suncream and the occasional real curiosity like a ball of grimy fat. ('Yes, it's yeti-fat. My sherpa gave it to me in the Himalayas one year – works wonders if your eyelids are beginning to go in a whiteout.')

Some skiers amass such a collection of bum-bag material that they graduate to the full skiing back-pack, as worn by guides and instructors. These are invaluable for denoting authority and are a worthwhile investment for all types of Survival Skier.

Whatever approach to gear you adopt, however, the basic rule is to have a lot of it – burdensome as this may be on the journey out. Even in this respect the extra effort involved will be more than compensated for by the lasting impression made on your fellow skiers if you travel out *en groupe*.

It is well worthwhile to invest in several pairs of skis of varying lengths. These can be picked up quite cheaply as most Continental or American skiers change their skis, on average, every twelve days. By contrast, British skiers, because of economic circumstances, are often forced to hang on to the same pair of skis for months at a time. It should be noted here that despite the money-no-object cachet attached to skiing, some Continental/American spending can be excessive; and if someone does persist in going on about their new micro-chip bindings and battery-operated centrally heated boots with built-in telephone and cocktail cabinet, there is surely no harm in remarking that in the end there is no substitute for good technique.

The Ski-Room

On arrival, when setting yourself up in the ski-room, your main aim should be to use your equipment to dominate as much of the room as possible. In addition to taking up plenty of storage space, you should try to establish a permanent working area for your waxes, portable burners, iron, clamps, files, scrapers and other assorted instruments.

An excellent space-taker which can almost serve as a landmark in 'your' sector is a pair of old ski-jumping skis. The only people who ever see these close to are championship ski-jumpers, and, in an ordinary hotel locker room towering above a forest of 175 cm compacts, they can have quite an unsettling effect on the competition. A pair of Scandinavian Fjell skis can be used to much the same effect. And you might as well have a pair of Scorpian mini-skis along with you 'just for fun'.

Don't just use the ski-room at the beginning and end of a day's skiing. If you can spare the time, three-quarters of an hour spent in the ski-room in the evening playing with your waxes and your implements can only enhance your reputation. You are sure to gather round you a small but respectful audience to whom you can explain the importance of a razor sharp 18 inches of inside edge under the boot.

Above all, take gear seriously. The Survival Skier should on no account admit that he doesn't ease the springs on his bindings from one year to the next. When

someone tells you that they ski so much better with the S26A5 binding than they did with the S26A4, or that they must be at least two per cent faster since they started wearing the latest wonder ski-socks, it is as well to believe them. You will win no friends by suggesting that the magic numbers and words written all over our skis, like 'elite', 'slalom' and 'competition' are simply there to make us feel good. Don't take these totems lightly. A man who has just spent a month's salary replacing his old 848 GTS Slalom Elite Specials with the improved 848 GTS Slalom Elite Extra-Specials is not likely to take kindly to having them mocked.

The only people who can sometimes get away with the deprecating approach to gear are the down-dressing Old-Timers. ('I remember how when I was a child we used to just strap a pair of barrel staves to our feet.') Only he can afford to be slightly irreverent in asking whether your bioelastic aerodynamic ski-suit really makes you ski faster, whether your shatter-sure hyper-reflectant sunglasses were specially designed for wearing on top of your head or whether your maximum angulation knee-high racing boots can possibly be more comfortable.

3. Bed and Board

'Sleep faster, we need the pillows'

Yiddish saying

Once you've picked your resort and got your gear, the next big decision is where to stay. In the Grand Hotel Vachement Cher or the Flophouse Familiale? In a Mod Cons Mountain Hut or Pack 'Em In Pension? Or perhaps in one of those modest establishments which seem to have sprung up behind most decent hotels these days, commonly known as The Annex. Wherever you end up, you can be sure that your home from home will have been designed to put Skiing Man to the test every bit as much as slopes.

Your *après-ski* hours will be full of little challenges, like trying to persuade the pension *patronne* to part with the bathroom key; discovering the half-hour in the day when the hot water is actually hot; sneaking upstairs past the receptionist wearing your ski-boots, in spite of all the notices saying you mustn't; working out how to adjust the heating in your room so that the temperature is somewhere between freezing and ferocious; or persuading the manager to move you out of the room next to the lift shaft or disco.

Not, of course, that all these little pleasures are exclusive to hotels in ski resorts. You probably have about as much chance of finding no coat-hangers or bath-plug or a fast-fading 15-watt bulb in your bedside reading lamp in a hotel at the bottom of the mountain as you would in one at the top. Nor do skiing hotels have a monopoly on switchboards which are *incommunicado* with the outside world, laundries that are guaranteed to savage your clothing, or chambermaids who are duty-bound to ignore your 'Do Not Disturb' sign.

However, it is true that skiing hotels are judged by different criteria from hotels down below. The three acid tests are:

a) size of breakfast
b) proximity to ski-lifts
c) the plumbing

In other words, do they give you an egg for your breakfast and enough to stoke up on for the rest of the day? Can you hear the clank and squeal of a nearby ski-tow when you wake up in the morning? Are the pipes noisy and do they offer a reasonable flow of hot water (neither trickle nor torrent) at the time of the day when you most need it?

It should be said, though, that these are tests applied more by Real Skiers than Survival Skiers, who are not usually as raring to go as they tend to make out.

There is often a certain masochistic streak in Real Skiers which can lead them to put up at some rotten hotel with no cons, let alone mod, on the grounds that it is a hotel 'for Serious Skiers'. In fact it's all a clever ploy by a hotelier who doesn't like being disturbed by his guests and has devised this way of attracting the 'early to bed, early to rise' crowd.

One quality common to all kinds of skier is that they are frequently skint. As we've seen, skiing can have serious side-effects on one's bank balance. This has meant that in today's hard times skiing accommodation is much affected by what is known as the Sardine Syndrome.

What this amounts to is more and more people staying in self-catering apartments and chalets and 'apartotels'. These are full of bunks and convertible couches and pull-down or fold-up beds which transform the place at night into one great dormitory where people can slumber amid the intoxicating odours of one another's socks drying out on the radiators.

If you're lucky there'll be a Chalet Girl to do the cooking. If not, there'll be a 'kitchenette' where you can heat up your own baked beans, which you then eat

sitting cross-legged on cushions in the area cleared during the daytime for communal activities.

There is something to be said for this lifestyle. Your booze (bought on the 'plane or from the supermarket) is cheaper than in the hotel bar. There are all the school dorm fun and games (pillow fights and tying people's pyjama legs together, and putting snow in their beds). And there's the constant challenge of trying to get into the bathroom.

But, on balance, the Survival Skier is advised to go for a more classical form of accommodation. This could be the quaint and cosy family-run Hotel Post (there's one in every village – all *Luftmalerei* and shutters outside, cuckoo clocks and doilies inside). Or it could be the ultra-modern over-equipped Hotel Sporting (often, for some mysterious reason, called the Hotel Golf, despite being perched on top of a mountain with no golf course for miles around).

What it will have, though, within its pine-clad walls, will be any number of saunas and solariums and pools (with whirlpools and underwater massage) and gymnasiums and games rooms and ski-wear shops and illuminated boards on the walls of the lobby showing all the *pistes*. All this and a sterilised polythene-wrapped tooth-glass in your bathroom, too.

This sort of place is often a good bet for the Survival Skier, who does need a certain amount of room for manoeuvre – a decent-sized ski-room to perform in, somewhere big enough to get lost in, and a selection of bars where he can sound off.

And even if the other skiers won't listen to you, there'll always be Mine Host or Hostess behind the bar busy with the cocktail shaker or brewing up the *Glühwein* while patiently lending an ear with well-feigned interest as you describe the local skiing terrain and your exploits upon it. (He or she will have been skiing this area since birth but don't let that hold you back.)

4. Ski-Talk

'The greater the lie, the more chance of it being believed'

Joseph Goebbels

This brings us to what is perhaps the Survival Skier's most vital requirement — the chat. For, as we've already remarked, skiing is a sport more for discussing than doing. It is not simply a question of making up for incompetence on the *piste* by grandiloquence off it. Ski-talk is definitely an acquired skill and there is probably more difference between novice and expert exchanging stories at the bar than there is between them on the slopes. One important point is that, initially anyway, you should try to confine your *braggadocio* to skiers of your own level.

Remember the unwritten code of mutual support among skiers which runs: 'You believe my stories and I'll believe yours. I won't go out the next day and look too hard for all the precipices, walls of death and giant man-eating moguls we spent last evening talking about.' However, this applies mainly among skiers of a similar ability. If you move up a couple of levels and try spinning the same yarns, you are likely to find undisguised contempt rather than the encouraging nods, the sucking in of breath, and the whistles of wonderment you can expect from your peers.

Styles of story-telling vary from level to level. The beginners' tales, for instance, are all breathless outpourings of hazards encountered, without much technical data: 'You know that ledge just by the baby T-bar, where everyone always falls on that big bump; well, I was doing a *schuss*, and really going, when, you know that woman with the red suit . . .'

The experts are more sparing and technical in their language, only pulling out the stops on a subject that clearly sets them apart from other groups (powder, for instance).

One general rule is that the tone of most ski conversations should be upbeat and enthusiastic. Your friends will not thank you for putting a dampener on their spirited accounts. Remember the basic convention of mutual acceptance of exaggeration and the need to be supportive.

An important part of this convention concerns accepted ratios of self-delusion. These should on no account be challenged. Most skiers, for instance, believe themselves to be travelling some 40 per cent faster than they actually are (for the novice this can be as high as 60 per cent). Do not attempt to put anyone right on this — you may find them doing the same for you.

Similar ratios apply to skiers' views of themselves in most other aspects of the sport. This may be a reason for the unpopularity of ski-schools which offer video as a teaching aid — filming pupils in action and then playing back the tape at evening self-criticism sessions. These are not usually well attended — most skiers clearly want to preserve their flattering misconceptions of themselves.

It is, of course, as true for skiing as for anything else that it's not what you say but the way you say it. Whatever the subject, whether it's gear, mountains, snow or technique, it's vital to dress it up in the right technical terms, ideally with key words being said in a foreign language. *'Wedeln'*, *'angulation'* and *'passo spinto'* all sound much better than 'wiggling', 'bending forward' and 'skating step'.

That is not to say that English has nothing to offer. The Americans have brought in a lot of good hot-dogging jargon in recent years – words like triple daffy, flamingo, spreadeagle, royal christies and backscratchers; not to mention doughnut, twister, wongbanger and helicopter.

Advice

The use of technical language both confirms your status as an experienced skier and has the advantage of being very flattering – even when you are discussing a comrade's weaker points. 'You're getting a lot of air through the moguls, John' is likely to be far more acceptable to John than 'You seem to be bouncing around out of control' or 'You don't seem to know how to handle bumps'.

Think twice before advising someone to 'Turn left and try to keep your balance'. He or she would much prefer 'Get an even weighting on your edges, then slide into maximum *angulation* to bring you round and flick your heels as you turn'.

When a novice skier lurches past you, struggling against the forces of gravity, say 'Hop, hop' or 'Go, go'. He will appreciate this more than 'Look out, you'll fall'.

The point is that the specialised vocabulary for what you are doing ('heel push using frictional gravity as you counter-rotate') sounds a lot better than what you are doing looks. Developing a facility for this kind of technical language and applying it liberally to your fellow skiers can be well worthwhile. You may feel you are spending an awful lot of time building up other people's egos, but in the end it pays. If people like what they hear about themselves they will tend to defer to you as the *maestro*.

Complex formulae and diagrams of forces are ideal for these conversations – either sketched out in the snow with your ski-stick or drawn in beer on the bar. Someone who can hold forth credibly on the appropriate mathematical formula for adjusting bindings for champagne powder as opposed to fluffy powder need probably do nothing more to establish a reputation.

The use of suitably obscure technicalities, however, can be a double-edged sword. While immensely flattering, if that's the intention, they can also serve as a put-down which can shatter another skier's morale.

The secret here is timing as much as tone. Obscure advice given *before* rather than after someone tries to execute a particular manoeuvre is almost certain to guarantee its failure. If that is, in fact, the aim, it's important for the advice to sound specific but really to be very vague. Above all, don't attempt to demonstrate. Just gaze on, shaking your head sadly as the victim tries to put the advice into practice and fails. This technique is commonly used to exclude a skier who is seeking to move into a higher league but is not showing the proper deference.

It is also important never to let your ski-talk lapse. Never say bump when you can say mogul or *bosse* instead. Never simply lose your balance and fall over — you catch an edge; you tried one slip turn too many; or you should have known better than to try a left-hand mogul before going into reverse camber.

It all helps to keep skiers cocooned in their own exclusive world and to enhance the general air of mystique. For skiers like to be in awe of their activity. They even apply their sense of wonderment to the inanimate objects which help them in their labours. They have reverent technical conversations about lifts, pylons and cable cars — idolising, in short, the whole range of teles (*télésiège, téléski, télébenne, télécabine,* etc.) that get them up the mountain.

People who would not spare a second thought for the engineering triumphs of the car or the aeroplane that got them to the resort in the first place, or to the construction of the skyscraper hotel in which they are lodging, will watch with undisguised awe as the cable car docks or pulls away. 'Just look at that', they will say excitedly to one another. 'It still hasn't taken up the strain on the third pulley. And that cabin must weigh at least three and a half tons!'

Amongst these inanimate objects you must certainly include mountains. Peak-worship is an important time-filler on the slopes and you can usually reckon that a good 25 per cent of the people on upper ski-slopes at any one time will be engaged in admiring, pointing out, identifying and making general obeisances to the surrounding mountain-tops.

You should not get too carried away, however. While it's important to use your terminology convincingly, the Survival Skier should be careful not to follow those people who actually begin to believe their own ski-talk and who feel there is a real relationship between what they say and what they do on the snow.

The ski neurotic has become a very familiar phenomenon on the slopes, worrying about whether his *angulation* might be a couple of degrees off or his skis five centimetres too long. (He's the one who studies his ski manual during the coffee break and anxiously consults the instructor after every lesson with questions like: 'Should I downweight on the uphill ski before or after I've reached maximum *angulation*?')

The ski neurotic has perhaps learned rather too well one of the basic lessons that all Survival Skiers have to master — that nothing is ever quite right. While it's true that the general tone of ski conversations is one of enthusiasm and excitement, they are invariably qualified by dissatisfaction with something or other. Either the equipment has not been set up right, or phases of certain manoeuvres are not coming off properly, or the snow conditions are wrong.

The Weather

Weather is one of the commonest gripes. The snow is never exactly as it should be. It has been perfect on nostalgically remembered occasions in the past, but it is never right *today*.

Make the most of this. Other skiers are always looking for something to blame and they'll be grateful if you can supply it. If someone is having a rough time on a perfectly prepared *piste*, he will be very happy if you suggest that although it

---

Rules of Skiing

WEATHER

The snow conditions are never right.

The snow reports are always wrong.

The weather always gets worse.

The weather in the village is never the same as the weather on the mountain.

The weather was better the week before you arrived.

You are never dressed to suit the day. You either sweat or you shiver.

The one day when snow conditions are ideal will be the day you decide to stay in bed.

The bumps are never in the right place.

If it's expected to snow, it won't.

If there isn't enough snow, there won't be any more.

looks easy, that sort of snow is very difficult to ski on. He will also welcome suggestions of other slopes where the snow may be better. Skiers are a bit like surfers, always willing to set off on that search for the perfect wave/slope, always fantasising about some mythical unskied dreamland of crisp, white powder.

Don't just talk about the weather. Get stuck in to it. Peer knowingly down crevasses. Point out potential avalanches. Put up a finger to test the wind. Taste the snow to examine its composition. And always shake your head and look dissatisfied.

It's also as well to be suitably reverential about the weather. For mountain weather is not to be thought of as ordinary weather — it's there to put you to the test. It can even put you to the test before you leave home; snow reports bear little relation to the truth and can take some deciphering.

Weather tends to be a big favourite with our friend the Old-Timer. He is always harking back to the great whiteouts of yesteryear, and other great battles against the elements.

The Way It Was

At this point it might be worth looking in more detail at how our Old-Timers apply themselves to ski-talk generally. They are often among the more effective exponents of the art and most of the principles they apply also hold good for other types of Survival Skier.

As already explained, the Old-Timers do a lot of their talking through their gear, which always looks suitably ancient. They fill out the picture with appropriate references to the old pre-cable days — leather thong bindings, home-made waxes and so on. Their dated equipment also has the advantage of providing a handy excuse should their performance on slope not seem immediately impressive. This doesn't happen all that often, though, as they are past masters at being seen outside as little as possible. They prefer to do most of their reputation-building work in the ski-room.

Their most common theme is that skiing has got too easy. So much of the challenge has been taken out of it. In the old days you used to have to endure to survive. Remember what it was like having to put on skins to get up a slope? Remember those ribbed hickory skis? And what about the early leather boots — you used to have to take them off every couple of hours and rub your feet in the snow to restore the circulation.

Working as he does mainly in the ski-room, the Old-Timer can easily make use of the full range of his props. He will drop in on a suitable ski-room conversation, choosing an appropriate moment to rummage around in his bum-bag allowing a number of intriguing items to spill out. It is not usually long before he is forced to explain about the seal gut used for binding fingers together in extreme cold and the whale-bone chips for propping eyes open in a blizzard.

Other Approaches

If the Old-Timer's line in chat doesn't appeal to you, you could base your own brand of ski-talk on the novice, who excuses himself by claiming to be more of a cross-country skier; the name-dropping member of the exclusive Club 8847 at Piz Lagalb; the adventure merchant ('Any Big Skiing around here?'); the latest technology buff, specialising in arcane talk about wedging; the hardened loner ('I spent most of the afternoon birdsnesting up over the top ridge); the skied-everywhere dilettante ('I like to do the Hahnenkamm-Streif once a year and usually try to make it for the Inferno at Mürren'); the low-profile Nature Lover ('I like getting in among the trees — did you know that slalom was originally a substitute for racing through woods?'); or the deckchair expert who never goes out at all ('I used to be a bit of a wall-skier until I lost my nerve').

Whatever role you adopt, the underlying precepts of ski-talk — a healthy disrespect for reality, mutual congratulation and flattery — remain the same at all levels. The only time when a somewhat different set of rules apply is in 'Anything you can do . . .' conversations. These are normally started by comparative novices who have rashly abandoned the conventions of mutual support. The Survival Skier should avoid such conversations at all costs as they often lead to an embarrassing escalation of claims.

If you do get involved, your aim should be to kill the conversation as early as possible. Our Old-Timer would probably trump his opponent with something like: 'Ever skied in Tibet? They have a curious sort of turn there — very similar to one I saw the natives in Patagonia using years ago.'

Finally, a little advice about pacing yourself. Whatever kind of ski-talker you are, it's important not to use up too much of your energy skiing during the day. You have to reach the bar in the evening with enough gusto left to tell your tale. You also, of course, need to keep something in reserve for your après-ski turns like the disco gyro and the bar-stool twirl.

Get your priorities right with regard to skiing and ski-talk. Never let your skiing impair your *après-ski* performance. A depressing day when you've skied yourself into the ground can so easily destroy your confidence and credibility. You need all the aplomb you can muster if you are to carry your ski-talk off.

5. Instruction and Group Skiing

'I trust I make myself obscure'

A Man For All Seasons

Up to now we have concentrated on those activities which will take up most of your time – basic *pre-* and *après-ski* work such as talking, shopping, posing and dressing up. But you will also have to spend a certain amount of time actually on the snow. Most of us, in fact, find ourselves strapping on the boards nearly every day.

When you do get out there you've two basic choices – skiing solo or *en groupe*. On the whole, Survival Skiers are advised to steer clear of classes. When you think about it, it really is a bit much to have to pay just to learn to slide downhill. Skiing is hard enough without some rubber-legged farm boy shouting at you all the time and without eight or ten other people being invited to sneer at your efforts. Can there really be any point in this chap, with no bones in his legs, teaching normal people with proper legs how to bend their knees? The answer is No. But it is one way of getting through the day and some people, even Survival Skiers, do seem to enjoy classes.

So let's look first at a typical ski-class in action. The group are lined up on a hillside, most of them facing the same way, listening, apparently attentively, as the instructor gives his lecture. There is no point, incidentally, in trying to understand the fellow. He's probably a goatherd by trade and he almost certainly won't speak much English – though he may have some Skinglish in the style of the American catch-phrase: 'Plant your pole, bend your knees, that'll be 50 dollars please.'

His patter is usually something along the lines of *'flexion . . . extension . . . planter les batons'*. Most pupils catch about every fifteenth word. The rest is lost because of the instructor's obscure pronunciation; or is drowned by the wind; or by the loudspeaker blaring out *Una paloma blanca*; or by the whispering of the two individuals in the group who think they know what the instructor is saying and have volunteered to translate. Don't listen to these people, by the way. They usually get the wrong end of the *baton*. In fact they are quite capable of missing the *baton* entirely and imagine, for instance, that an instructor talking about *'cannes'* is talking about his holidays in the South of France. Whatever the instructor says, actually, doesn't much matter. He talks mainly to give the class a breather and to make him feel he's doing his job properly. For him, this is the hard part.

Next comes the demonstration. The instructor executes a series of turns or exercises while the group all ooh and aah to each other and say 'Doesn't he make it look easy'. The class then proceed to make their own way down, one by

---

Rules of Skiing

PROGRESS

You won't be able to understand the instructor.

The older or less comprehensible the instructor, the more talking he will do.

Whatever it is you are doing wrong, the instructor will probably tell you to bend your knees more.

Most people don't think they are in quite the right class for their class of skiing. Very few think they should move down a class.

All skiers are aiming to reach a particular level of skiing ability where they imagine their problems will be over. No-one ever does.

The turn you learned last year will be out of fashion this year.

Whenever you think you are getting the hang of it, you are doing it wrong.

Several times during your holiday you will ask yourself: 'Why am I doing this?'

Each year you learn about as much as you've forgotten since the year before.

---

one, starting off at the instructor's signal. If you are somewhere like Austria the group will do as it's been told and peel off from the top of the line. If you are somewhere like Italy the starting order is likely to be the subject of some discussion, but will in the end be totally random. You can also be sure that at some point two members of the class will attempt to set off at the same moment.

The main point to note, though, is that whatever manoeuvre the instructor has performed, the class is unlikely to make any concession to it. They will all ski down in exactly the same way as they always do, each with his or her own distinctive style – rolling the shoulders, sticking out the bottom in the classic potty position or failing to plant the pole.

While the members of the class perform their specialities, the instructor usually amuses himself by chatting up a passing female. He breaks off briefly as each pupil arrives to explain how he or she should be doing more *flexion*, more *extension* or more planting of the *batons*. He then gives the signal for the next pupil to come down and resumes his conversation with the girl. To be fair, as everyone always comes down the same way it doesn't really matter whether he watches them or not.

The whole exercise will then be repeated. The class regroups, the instructor gives his lecture, demonstrates a different movement and skis down until he disappears out of sight beyond the brow of a hill. He then waves his stick in the air, a member of the class spots the tip of it poking up in the distance and the class proceeds to come down one by one, exactly as before. Occasionally, the whole class will go down together – usually after discussing, at some length, whether this was or was not what the instructor intended. The only real change, though, might be that this time the instructor is talking to a different girl.

There will be times when your group will contain a girl who is sufficiently desirable to interest the instructor. In this case she will normally perform first, carefully watched by him. She will then be given a 20-minute commentary on the progress she is making, plus any help she may need at adjusting her gear, and possibly an offer of a private lesson in Duvet Skiing. The others will then follow on down in quick succession while he continues to entertain her, breaking off as each of her classmates arrives for a quick word on more *flexion*, *extension* or planting of the *batons*.

When the instructor decides it's time for a change of pace he will lead you all on a long knee-slamming run, probably over an area of corrugated hardpack. The critical formula for the Survival Skier here is *'après vous'*: try to go last and make sure the group does not go off in an orderly fashion. As people fall you can then stop and ask them if they are all right. This gives you a chance to take a breather and earns you a reputation as a solid type. If, by some mischance, nobody falls, you can easily bring down the person in front of you by skiing on his or her heels.

Usually, however, the instructor will ensure that mishaps take place. In order to maintain his superiority he will have chosen a piece of ground that only he can properly negotiate. Ski instructors have a vested interest in making you ski badly, if only to prove that you are in need of instruction. It's a favourite trick of theirs to ski a bit too fast or a bit too slow to enable you to perform properly on a given piece of ground. Even though instructors vary a good deal there are no exceptions to the rule that power corrupts. And the most likely victim of their tyrannical streak is undoubtedly the Survival Skier with his probable recalcitrance and incompetence.

If it becomes apparent that the instructor wants to take it out on you ('Why you always fall?') there is no reason to be intimidated. You are perfectly free to ask him when he's got to go off and milk the cows. Don't feel obliged to show the sort of fawning deference that most pupils go in for. The worst he can do is deprive the group of essential items of equipment, like sticks, and make them ski down in silly ways. You can also get your own back by reminding him that those who can, do and those who can't, teach. Most of these lads once saw themselves as the Killy, Stenmark or Thoeni of their neck of the woods but never made it into the big league.

It is perhaps worth mentioning that the real Killys, Stenmarks and Thoenis of this world do cause considerable problems for your humble tutor. This is because the instructors, like us, are the victims of the pet theories of the people who can really ski. If, for example, next year you find yourself being solemnly taught to lift the rear of your trailing ski on the turn, it will be because one of the top racers has sparked off a fashion by winning races that way. The superstars are the ones who really move ski technique on, forcing the establishment to keep on rewriting all the manuals and issuing new sets of instructions. These are supposed to apply to you and me but, as we just tend to ski on as we have always done, it tends to be the poor instructors who get most confused by it all.

All this explains why one year you get told to keep your skis together all the way through your parallel and the next that you'd do better to keep them eight inches apart; or why one year you are supposed to hop both skis around simultaneously and another to do most of your work on the outside leg, lifting and sliding the inside one round to join it. Not that any of this has much effect; if you watch a busy ski-slope for a while you will see that there are almost as many styles as there are people. Not even the instructors ski in the same way.

In fact, if you could ski a little faster, your particular variation would probably stand as much chance of becoming the new orthodoxy as did Killy's little quirks. The jet turn became acceptable because Jean-Claude started winning with it. The scissors turn, now as redundant as its high jump equivalent, could become *de rigueur* tomorrow if you started beating the world with it. We would surely all find ourselves going back to the Arlberg crouch if someone came along who could do it a little better than they could in the 1920s. If you won the Olympic Downhill chewing gum, they'd all soon be chewing away on the slopes. So, next time the instructor goes on about your excessive shoulder-rolling, point out that what you are doing is really a primitive version of shoulder swings or mambo, now found in all the best textbooks.

Instructors, however, are not usually very tolerant of individualism. The only time they are slightly indulgent towards eccentricity is when confronted with someone who's obviously from an earlier skiing era — like our old-time ski-tourer. If you are playing this role, you can usually enlist the instructor's sympathy for your unorthodoxy by saying you just can't get out of what is basically a Telemark action. You're reasonably safe here because none of the instructors have much idea what a Telemark actually looked like. The instructor may indeed even develop a sort of respect for you and be reluctant to break this link with the past. If he tries, just shrug your shoulders and say: 'Once a Telemarker, always a Telemarker — I just can't get the hang of this modern technique.' If you try this approach always remember to refer to the instructor as a guide.

The principal advantage of these tactics is that you don't have to start from scratch again every year. For even though it now takes seven days instead of

seven years to become a skier, you have to go back to the beginning every holiday because a new method has evolved in the intervening year. It often seems as if there's a conspiracy among ski-schools always to keep technique one jump ahead of the pupils.

Whatever theory your instructor goes for, he will almost certainly have a repertoire of catch-phrases which vary little from year to year. Many relate to a particular part of your anatomy that is supposed to be the key to it all. Thus we get:

> *'Ski-lauf ist Knie-lauf.'*
> 'You ski with your head.'
> 'You ski with your big toe.'
> 'You ski with your nose.'
> 'Grip the snow with your toes.'

Italian and French instructors are also rather fond of sexual references, usually, of course, directed at the instructor's favourite girl in the class:

'Skiing is like making love – easy when you get the hang of it.'

Instructors are also inclined to keep evoking that mythical beast, the Fall Lion, which, strangely enough, you are always advised to turn into and attack even though it will always bring you low.

Your tutor may also have a penchant for drawing immensely complex diagrams in the snow, usually for the benefit of a particular member of the group. 'Kennst du ein Bisschen Mechanik?' he will say and proceed to detail the plethora of forces acting on you at any one time.

To vary the pace a bit, the instructor will sometimes stop to admire the view or pass round some saucisson and white wine for refreshment. How long this takes tends to depend on the interest shown by the aforementioned girl in the names of mountains or the varieties of local vino. Needless to say, it's as well to encourage her to show an interest. Any time the group goes up by T-bar, by the way, it will always be the instructor who goes up with the girl.

Another variation is to break things up with slalom practice. This can be quite fun and is not necessarily all that strenuous. It is usually a good time-waster as it involves preparing the course. This means fetching the sticks, planting them at appropriate intervals and then spending time side-slipping or snow-ploughing down to smooth out the course. It is not too hard to bow out of the slalom itself by claiming some religious objection to competition. Anyway, people are always needed to tidy up the course and put back the sticks that get knocked down, so you can remain involved with the proceedings by doing that. To get the maximum benefit from all this you must insist on the class taking the time and trouble to set up its own course – some instructors have an unfortunate tendency to 'borrow' courses set up by another group.

Selecting Your Class

This is one of the reasons why it's worth choosing your instructor very carefully at the start of the week. Don't let the ski-school make this important decision for you. If the school organises one of the usual mass selection sessions, getting everyone to go through their tricks so they can sort you into classes, make a point of being absent. If challenged you can say you were delayed because you had to make some vital adjustment to your gear. Then, when it's all over, you just latch on to the class that suits you best.

You may as well abandon any notions you may have of a sort of logical progression in skiing. There is simply no point in progressing just for the sake of it. It's best to find a level you like and stick to it. If you are happiest traversing, pick a class that does nothing but. If you enjoy stemming, always seek out the stem class.

People are often misled by the apparently hierarchical nature of the sport, divided, as it is, into groups ranked on a scale from one to six. You will find, however, that in practice there is very little difference between the grades. It's just that each class is nominally engaged in a different series of manoeuvres as they carry on assiduously practising their faults.

One class to avoid, though, is the beginners' class. The disadvantage here is that they are not allowed to use the lifts much, so you have to do an awful lot of rather exhausting walking uphill. All that snow-ploughing can also be rather tiring.

Some people, it is true, do engage in *après-ski* one-upmanship based on the number of your class. But if you do get picked on in this way, it's usually fairly easy to cloud the issue, given that countries vary in their ranking systems. In France, for instance, class one is the top class and class six for beginners, whereas in Italy it is the other way round.

Classmates

Finally, a word about your classmates. You can be sure that most of them will not take such a rational view of things as the Survival Skier who just slots himself into the most accommodating class. Instead they will worry a great deal about where their class is ranked in the general scheme of things, and where they rank in the class scheme of things. Most will believe that their talents are undervalued and that they have been put into the wrong class. 'But I've done all this', they will say, regardless of whether they are still able to do it, or indeed whether they were ever able to do it. 'I mean, we were on to pedal-jump turns last year.' When giving vent to such expressions of dissatisfaction they will always hark back to some Golden Age when their parallels (sic) were out of this world. It all comes down to that capacity for self-delusion which most skiers have and which often makes it all so amusing. Try watching someone who thinks he's doing a *wedel* but isn't.

The Survival Skier is best advised to support his fellow pupils in their beliefs, although there are always one or two who are beyond the pale as far as expressions of sympathy or solidarity are concerned. There is, for example, the chap who always insists on being the first to perform and who, when you are skiing as a group, monopolises the Number Two spot behind the instructor. He invariably feels he should be at least a couple of classes higher up and that bagging the Number Two spot reflects his status in the class. There is, incidentally, no advantage to be had from being the best in the class — it just means the instructor will find even more to criticise.

The chap who is convinced he's a real bomber is even more of a menace. He never follows the rest of the class in their attempts to weave a curved path behind the instructor. He hurtles straight down, usually parallel to the group but sometimes across its path, huddled up in his version of the egg position, clearly imagining he's doing the Kilometro Lanciato. He usually arrives breathless, about half a second before the rest of the group, expecting to be congratulated. When skiing down to join the group, he will never ski past and tack on to the group from below. Instead, he tries one of his racing stops, aiming to fall in at the top of the line but invariably crashing and collapsing the whole group like a row of dominoes.

Whatever differences they may have during class, most groups manage to put up a common front to the outside world during *après-ski* time. They will all rally round and back each other up on stories about the arduous and extensive skiing they have been doing.

Most instructors realise how important a conversation piece the group's travels are, so they usually endeavour to move the class around as much as possible in the course of a day. Thus, when asked that standard dinner-time question, 'Where did you go this afternoon?' you have no difficulty in replying:
'Well, we went up the Black Buzzard and down the White Crow at least 15 times. Then we skied over to the Spitzenspitze, did the Wall of Death a few times, then took that long double drag which connects with the Devil's Cauldron. Up there we found a superblack with no-one on it at all, skied it half a dozen times and then bombed down to Hochgurgl; from there we went over to Obergurgl, down to Untergurgl and finally took the cable car to Übergurgl just in time to catch the last lift back.'

6. Solo Piste Bashing

'If you don't have it in your head, you have it in your legs'

Serbian Proverb

'The Survival Skier should reverse this'

Author

Most Survival Skiing techniques are, in fact, better suited to individual *piste* bashing than to group skiing. It has already been made clear that the Survival Skier usually relies on not making himself too conspicuous. He knows he's only as good as his last turn in public and, to ensure that these are few and far between, he will have picked terrain with plenty of cover, a variety of interlinked ski areas and lots of escape routes.

A properly prepared Survival Skier should never find himself in a situation where he is forced to perform under the critical gaze of others. If necessary, he can outwait anyone on the mountain and he has plenty of time-wasting props at his disposal — camera, suntan cream, screwdriver, waxes, map and so on.

Above all, the Survival Skier will rely on what's called 'just off *piste*' technique — basically the art of standing around beside the *piste* in any one of a number of suitable poses. Probably the most common position is to lean back, perhaps supported by the ski-sticks, arms folded, glasses on head and eyes closed, facing the sun. In the absence of sun the poser might be looking out across country, scanning the neighbouring peaks, marvelling at Mother Nature.

Alternatively, he can go in for a somewhat more active routine, like shuffling off to inspect some nearby unskied powder. That doesn't commit him to skiing in it — he can always come back and say he hasn't got the right kind of wax handy.

The average Survival Skier can do a lot to develop his standing about technique by just watching and imitating the Real Skier. For although attempts to emulate the motions of good skiers in action are almost certainly doomed to failure, their motions when more or less stationary can be copied very successfully.

The most common expert postures tend to depend on ways of leaning backwards or forwards or sideways on the sticks. There is also a good deal of simulation of skiing positions — bending the knees, leaning into imaginary turns and so on. Other characteristic routines are standing still, stork-like, holding the back of one ski off the ground or, by contrast, making impatient little bunny hops. For relaxation, there's sitting down or lying back on the skis, sometimes flexing oneself into a semi-prone limbo position. Skis are kept together throughout, of course. But whereas keeping them together leads to disaster while skiing, you will be surprised how easy it is when you are not moving.

Rules of Skiing
GETTING AROUND

If you start out in the morning 15 minutes later than usual, you will arrive on the slopes an hour later than usual.

The most exhausting part of skiing is getting from the hotel to the slopes.

Skis and ski-boots weigh more at the end of the day than at the beginning.

Most skiers give themselves away by how they carry their skis to and from the slopes.

When you set out from one point on the mountain to another which appears to be on the same level, it will turn out to require much tramping uphill.

A more energetic way of hanging around is to go in for on-the-spot exercises. There are a variety of these, but perhaps the best are the ones which involve using the sticks in an imaginative manner. You can pick up some interesting examples by watching a German or Scandinavian group at one of their early morning knees-bend sessions or, even better, an Inner Skiing ('*Ski Psychologique*') class in action.

It goes without saying that all of this activity is best undertaken on a flat piece of ground. You will be surprised at how many movements which are impossible while steaming down a slope can be elegantly executed when you are on the level. Ability to make good use of the flat is one of the main characteristics of the successful Survival Skier.

But however accomplished your 'just off *piste*' technique you can't, of course, stand still for ever. So when the time comes to move off, pick your moment carefully. Don't hesitate to condescendingly '*après vous*' anyone who tries to nudge you into action before you are ready.

Starts can be difficult and very revealing, so a growing number of Survival Skiers are putting a lot of effort into perfecting imitations of the starting style of Real Skiers. This usually involves choosing the steepest slope available to gain immediate momentum and then casually falling into the first turn, adjusting the straps of the ski-sticks around the wrists at the same time.

Some Survival Skiers can even do a catapult racing start, jumping skis off the snow and pushing off with the sticks as if leaping out of a starting gate. A lot of practice is needed to get this off properly, but it can be worth it. It's another example of how, by working hard on a limited repertoire of special manoeuvres, one can enhance one's reputation as a skier without actually skiing.

To get about on the *piste* our Survival Skier will rely principally on traversing. So, having performed his super-start, he may possibly execute just one turn before sliding into his habitual traverse/sideslip position, tracking across country looking suitably detached until he finds another appropriate vantage point or convenient hostelry. Many Survival Skiers, in fact, spend the day traversing from refreshment stop to refreshment stop. This can make them a bit of a liability to other skiers when they roll down the main concourse to catch the last lift down at the end of the day.

If you feel that almost constant use of the traverse doesn't seem quite the thing after your professional 'just off *piste*' performance and flying start, the best face-saver is to look worried and keep stopping. It's a good general rule anyway to be constantly fiddling with your gear, adjusting it and complaining. So simply traverse off as if you are about to launch into a spectacular run and suddenly pull up short, looking puzzled, as if something is wrong. Then traverse on till you find a suitable spot and start making some vital adjustment to your equipment.

On no account allow yourself to get carried away by your own 'just off *piste*' performance. Don't be tempted to try to imitate some *Pistenjaeger* who has followed his flying start with a quick *wedel* through the powder at the edge of the *piste*. The accomplished Survival Skier must be aware of his limitations. Stick to the traverse. It's easy to execute, looks elegant enough and, with a bit of practice, the Survival Skier can perform it almost as well as the expert. And don't overdo the banana or comma position: some instructors get their pupils to hold the sticks out like a *banderillero* and this really does look as if you are trying too hard.

The great thing about the traverse, apart from being easy to execute, is that it does carry you across and away, rather than down. This means you can usually stay well clear of the main action and, since you are generally up on the valley sides, you also appear appropriately aloof from the proceedings.

However well you plot your evasive course you are almost bound, on occasion, to run across a group of people you know. Your approach here will vary according to their skiing ability, but in general it's a good idea to get in first and suggest that they are the ones who have been making themselves scarce all day: 'Ah, there you are — and where have you been hiding?' Try to stop beside them as sedately as you can. If you've been traversing this can usually be done by simply turning uphill to run out. Then get to work putting some of your standing around technique into practice. Unless they really know what they are doing, you can afford to remain somewhat detached, standing aside from the group and nodding encouragingly if they start practising their turns.

It's usually wise to let them go off first, but if they show no signs of moving pick a suitable moment and just traverse on, adopting your best 'seen it all, done it all' expression. Unless you happen to be hopelessly lost, never be tempted to join one of these groups. If you should have to for some reason, make sure you go last and then peel off at the earliest possible opportunity.

7. Queues

'E pur si muove'

Galileo Galilei

So far we have looked at how to get down the slope and how best to make use of stops *en route*. But the true secret of Survival Skiing is to ensure that you spend most of your day going not downhill, but uphill – or rather, attempting to go uphill. You will, in fact, spend most of your time queuing – so much so that a skiing holiday often seems like a misnomer for a queuing holiday.

Some people even spend as much time before they go on holiday studying the queuing facilities (checking there are bars nearby, that queues are south-facing) as they do studying the slopes. This sort of detail is, of course, very important to Survival Skiers who depend a lot on queues.

It's as well, therefore, to be wary of some of the newer purpose-built resorts which seem to be doing their best to eliminate queuing. This is a pity as skiing would not be skiing without the queuing. Think of all those magic moments spent shuffling forward, getting new designs scratched on to your skis by other skis, and exercising your elbows.

There are many Survival Skiers whose queue technique is well in advance of their slope technique. Indeed, there are some who find meeting the challenges offered in the ski queue far more rewarding than performing on the slopes. It would be a pity if all the years spent perfecting their technique were to go to waste should queuing ever disappear.

Queuing, of course, is an activity particularly well-suited to the English, who get a lot of practice at home, and who don't mind getting their skis scraped since they usually rent their equipment. Living up to their reputation for fair play, they are among the best at spotting and denouncing the Queue Sneak. These loathsome individuals are normally to be found trying to slide past on the outside, which is where the queue moves fastest anyway, or pushing through the middle pretending they are with someone further on.

Some like to sit innocently on the railings at the side of the queue and slide along a metre or so when no-one's looking. There are also a good many who have no hesitation in making straight for the front of the queue. They either say they are with a special group up ahead or that they lost control when stopping and found themselves at the head of the queue. Some just bribe the lift man to turn a blind eye to their activities.

The important thing is to challenge them early enough. It's not much good coming out with: 'I say, I was before you' once it's all a *fait accompli*. Nothing is a surer confession of impotence. Your best bet is to get the crowd on your side before challenging the Queue Sneak. Whip up a general feeling of indignation

Rules of Skiing

LIFTS AND LINES

The other queue moves faster.
Someone will try to jump the queue.
Someone will stand on the back of your skis.
You will stand on the back of someone else's skis.
Whenever you assume the attendant won't want to see your lift pass, he will.
The attendant will only ask to see your lift pass just as you're about to step on to the lift.
Someone will fall off the tow.
The other tow moves faster.
If there are two tows running parallel, one will break down.
You will always be on the one that breaks down.
If the tow stops and you abandon it, it will start to run again almost immediately.

and if possible prompt someone else to take the lead in denouncing the offender. Then come in as the back-up man: 'That's right, mate, you tell him.'

Once war has been declared, the confrontation usually turns into an interesting tussle of wills. Some sneaks quite shamelessly stand their ground, but others can be made to retreat, though not necessarily right to the back. They often manage to save face by reinserting themselves into the queue half way down.

If you can spot the sneak early enough, it is much more likely to be a straightforward physical contest. Don't hesitate to use force. This is one of the reasons for having ski-sticks. The proverbial poke in the eye with a sharp stick can be an excellent deterrent, although unfortunately very pointed poles are now being outlawed at some resorts. You can also use your sticks for blocking someone's way or to pin down their skis until you can plant your own skis on top of theirs. Sharp elbows and rugby-style hand-offs are also very useful. A certain amount of goose-stepping in the lift queue can also pay dividends.

Don't be afraid to use any of these weapons on children. They are the worst sneaks of the lot, usually attacking in groups and often wearing crash helmets to protect them from blows to the head. Despite the smiling indulgence these brats will be shown by some members of the queue — presumably those with similar offspring — make sure you stand your ground. These wowsers will be the *piste* beasts of the next generation. Now is your chance to settle scores with them. Don't be intimidated just because they can ski better than you.

8. Going Up

'Ski slopes are great places for running into people'

Snoopy

Every good queue eventually comes to an end and when you reach it you'll probably find a tele-something-or-other to transport you uphill.

There's an astonishing variety of teles, but the most common is probably some sort of drag-lift. So the Survival Skier needs to devote a good deal of time to developing his *tire-fesse* technique. The way you slide on and off the drag and just how you allow yourself to be hauled up can be very revealing.

This is particularly true of T-bars, where you usually go up with somebody else, thus providing you with an unrivalled opportunity to vent your skimanship on a captive audience.

Unless you know otherwise, it is best immediately to assume you are the senior partner. If your companion really is a novice it makes things very easy. You can offer encouraging looks, tell them to relax and be generally patronising. Always let the other person make the important choices — like who should get off first at the top. Try to seem indifferent towards the whole thing — except for the odd worried look if your partner seems unsteady at any point.

If your companion does not seem to accept your captainship, try to talk or frighten him or her into submission. A good start is to give advice about snow conditions. The weather is one of the standard topics in T-bar conversations. Point out remote mountains and perhaps more obscure geographical features. Turn around a lot to look back. Jiggle about on the bar. Swap hands with your sticks. Steer wide to avoid bumps or dips. Rummage through all your pockets in search of lip salve or cigarettes and then get your companion to hold your gloves while you cream or light up. Do anything, in fact, to unsettle your partner. Don't allow yourself to be side-tracked by the so-called 'romance of the T-bar'.

Another good idea is to make patronising remarks about good skiers who pass you on their way down. There are usually a few talented performers who enjoy bombing down immediately alongside the tow. Shake your head sadly when some supreme *wedel* artist flashes past and say something like: 'I'm sure that boy had potential . . . once. He'll never get rid of those bad habits now!'

If at the top there is any sort of pile-up or confusion — whether caused by you or otherwise — stick to the same drill as for motoring accidents. Assume it's someone else's fault and curse about the number of incompetent novices about. You'll probably get away with it, as the rules about who does what at the top of T-bars are far less clear than the Highway Code.

It's also a good idea to extricate yourself as quickly as possible from any *mêlée*. That way you can use the other bodies to lever yourself up. If you end up as the

Rules of Skiing

FALLING

Falling isn't fun.

The more you fall, the more you are likely to fall.

The closer you ski to the fall line, the more likely you are to fall. That's why it's called the fall line.

You are most likely to fall when someone you know is watching.

Most falls will be blamed on equipment, the snow or someone else.

If you put two novice skiers well apart on an empty slope, at some point on their way down they will collide.

The skier you most want to see fall never does.

last one on the ground you can have a hard time getting on your feet.

When you go up a drag-lift solo, rather than *à deux*, a different approach is called for. Here your performance is for the benefit of the world at large, not another individual. Use the opportunity to mask your skiing incompetence by showing off one or two eye-catching manoeuvres you have perfected.

Simple examples include all kinds of snappy ways of carrying or trailing the ski-poles. Some people like to flick the snow with them. Somewhat more advanced is the rhythmic swaying motion, so that you go up in a series of S-bends, interspersed with shuffling or leaning forward on your sticks which are planted somewhere in your bindings. For the very advanced, there's a technique of catching an edge so that you sway sideways and trail one ski behind you across the track for a while before hauling yourself back on course.

If you slip up on a drag-lift, the best thing is to pretend you were doing the *pisteurs'* job for them and smoothing over a bumpy bit. As you stagger to your feet, mutter to the people coming past you: 'Well, at least that hole won't be bothering anyone else for a while.'

When it comes to cable cars and cabins you depend less on actions and more on that Survival Skier's speciality – words. The talk tends to revolve around gear since you have to take your skis off and are usually huddled together as you wait. Thus everyone has the chance to inspect what everyone else is wearing or carrying at rather close quarters.

These are often the times when you realise how battle-scarred your skis have become and decide that you need a new pair. It is also when someone with short skis will be made to feel markedly inferior. Stare contemptuously at anyone with compacts or mini-skis. These are the big giveaway and no Survival Skier can afford to take them seriously. If you happen to have a pair you'll have to try to pretend you borrowed them.

Although opportunities for action are limited in cable cars, they are not completely excluded. One highly successful Survival Skier has even managed to build his whole reputation around a well-rehearsed trick at the middle station of a bubble-lift. It involves leaving his skis at the middle station the night before so that he can then stage his little drama when he collects them the next morning. As his cabin approaches the middle station, he opens the doors from the inside by forcing a ski-stick between them and turning the locking lever outside. Then, as the cabin passes slowly through the middle station transferring from one cable to another, he jumps out, grabs his skis, stuffs them into the empty ski-holder and rejoins his three bemused companions in the bubble. To maximise the value of this ploy he arranges to travel up with a different group of people every day.

All this depends, of course, on the connivance of the lift men at the middle station, and it costs him a bottle of Glenfiddich a week. Never underestimate the importance of keeping in with officials and the value of a good bribe. Always make a point of shaking hands with these chaps. Even if they don't know you, they will pretend to recognise you — they know an accomplished Survival Skier when they see one.

The advantage of developing one of these more elaborate gambits is that once you have it taped there is very little else you need do. In fact, it is positively unwise to do much else. There is, for instance, one very successful Survival Skier whose whole reputation rests on the fact that as he skis down to stop outside an hotel or restaurant he gives a little jump and manages to flick himself out of his bindings, boots together, to land neatly a couple of feet away from his skis. His bindings, of course, have to be on a very loose setting, but this doesn't matter as he doesn't ever ski. He just comes up to the slopes twice a day to perform his trick. The point, though, is that he has got his act off to perfection. He spent a whole year practising it in his back garden before trying it out on the slopes.

By contrast, there are other Survival Skiing techniques which can also make a lasting impression but which require hardly any practice at all. Try skiing down carrying ski-pickets or flags or some other piece of equipment over your shoulder. It's surprisingly easy to do but it looks deceptively difficult to the majority of people who never have occasion to try it.

Even something as simple as wearing a pack on your back (preferably one of those red ones used by Austrian instructors) can help to establish seniority — particularly if you offer to carry things for other people in it. If they take you up on the offer use the opportunity to show off the compass and map and other bits and pieces you keep inside.

You don't always need to actually possess the props. Often all you need do is refer to some of the items at hand on the slopes. For example, some Survival Skiers like to remark whenever they see a blood wagon: 'Ever tried pulling one of those?' If anyone comes back with 'No' and then an impertinent 'Have you?', our Survival Skier is ready to bluff it out with something like: 'It's okay if you've got the weight right and have someone behind who knows what he's doing.'

However well practised your routines are, though, you are bound on occasion to come a cropper and end up with your nose, or some other part of your anatomy, in the snow. There are all manner of possible face-saving remarks, but perhaps the most satisfactory are those that suggest you were attempting something very difficult which did not in this instance quite come off. You were, for example, practising your 'recovery skiing' but didn't manage to get back on the rails this time. Or you were working on your snow-shoe walking technique ('It's difficult to do on skis, of course, but very good exercise'). Or you were doing your bit for nostalgia by trying the old one-stick Zdarsky swing.

Don't hesitate to blame your equipment: 'I made a mistake with the wax and they just stick at all the wrong moments.' Claim that *Schnee* magazine asked you to test out some new bindings to see how suitable they would be for Mr Average. Or pretend you are on very unsuitable ultra-modern equipment ('That's the trouble with this high technology gear — may be okay for wind tunnels, but not on the slopes').

A final word on falling: when you do go try to make it as spectacular as possible. As in judo, tumbles are well worth practising. If you go down in a mushroom cloud of snow, people may assume, particularly if you help them to, that you were doing something rather ambitious. On the other hand, if you just wobble along and quietly sit down sideways after staring at your ski-tips and making them cross, you are not very likely to be given the benefit of the doubt. And don't be deluded by all those brochure pictures of a smiling lass collapsing into the powder that suggest falling is fun. It isn't.

9. Avoidance Skiing

'Include me out'

Sam Goldwyn

Although most Survival Skiers find themselves spending their time *piste* bashing, there is, for the really advanced, another possibility – Avoidance Skiing. The purest form – TAS (Total Avoidance Skiing) – means not going out at all. This, however, is only for those very exceptional types who can say 'Don't know if I could ski or walk first' and leave no doubt in people's minds that they are telling the truth.

It's no good the average performer thinking he can bow out by pleading a 'dicky cartilage' or even by trying something more ambitious like 'Never been much good since I split my shin on the Eiger'. He just won't be allowed to get away with it.

But it is possible to spend a day 'out skiing' without putting in much of an appearance *en piste*. This usually means slipping away via some little known route, usually off *piste*. You then go to ground in some mountain hideaway beyond the main skiing areas and spend your day sampling the landlord's *Glühwein*, usually in the company of other Avoidance Skiers.

Much depends, though, on first-rate preparation. Since no-one is going to catch sight of you on the slopes you must work very hard to establish and explain yourself before setting out. This means that at the hotel ski-room or the main departure point on the mountain you'll have to talk loud and long about the joys of skiing in the wilderness. Your gear, of course, will reflect this taste for getting off the beaten track. You wouldn't go far wrong with the sort of garb worn by our Old-Timer.

Incidentally, this communal preparation for the day's endeavours is one of the principal skiing rituals, as is the story-swapping off-with-the-boots session on returning to base in the evening.

The sort of line the Avoidance Skier will take is fairly obvious:

● 'Don't go in much for this *piste* bashing. Always was more of an endurance skier. Like to get stuck into the heavy stuff!'
● 'Never ski down the same hill twice if I can help it!'
● 'Always was more of a cross-country skier – like to get away from things, you know!'
● 'I prefer to get lost somewhere – never could stand much waiting around in lift queues.'

The drawback of Avoidance Skiing is that to escape you nearly always have to go off *piste*. As a result there is a danger of running into trouble and finding

Rules of Skiing

LOSSES

Every day, you will
a) forget something; b) break something; c) lose something

This is most likely to be
a) your lift pass; b) sunglasses; c) ski pole basket

If you lose a ski or a stick in deep snow, you will never find it where you thought you lost it.

The chances of losing any given item are in direct proportion to its importance and replaceability.

You never manage to lose the item you most want to lose so that you can justify buying a swanky new one.

You won't remember after lunch where it was outside that you left your skis.

yourself limping back to civilisation looking like the abominable *Homo Nivium* emerging from a snow war. But if you have the gall you can sometimes turn the situation to advantage with remarks like:

- 'Been practising my avalanche technique – it's fun trying to stay ahead when they break!'
- 'I was cruising around looking for a good avalanche and one found me!'
- 'Ever done any stunt skiing?'
- 'I think next time I'll play it safe, take out my ballet skis and quietly practise my royal christies.'
- 'I always was stronger at the shooting side of biathlon.'

Should anyone be intrigued enough to try to follow the Avoidance Skier, they can usually be put off with: 'If you try it, old boy, stay clear of the crevasses. You can usually feel the texture of the snow change, but not always . . .'

This spine-chilling approach is worth developing. It only needs the odd remark to create a picture of a wilderness beyond the *piste* full of bodies buried in drifts or impaled on trees. Try:

- 'What's your crevasse rescue drill like?'
- 'I was really looking for a spot of *couloir* skiing – I need a bit of a challenge these days!'
- 'I went over the top this morning. There's some real over-the-head Rocky Mountain-type powder in the dips.'

The odd reference to helicopters does no harm: 'Pity there's no heli-skiing around here!' (Be sure to check first that there is none.) Some people need do no more than say 'I ski alone' to conjure up a vision of a hardened loner with a phial of morphia in his bum-bag.

But there are less hazardous ways of Avoidance Skiing. One approach, if you can get up early enough, is to catch the first lift up (being careful to stay clear of any early morning German skiers or even the occasional group of hearty 'first run' Brits) and then appear back in the ski-room to wind up your day just as the others are getting ready. You then proceed to tell them, sounding as exhilarated as you can, that for you there's only one time of day when the mountain is at its best. That's the early morning. And for someone who wants to work on their ice or powder technique there's no better time. Snow conditions can be so interesting early in the morning and it's such a pleasure to be off *piste* when all the animals wake up. Once you've established all this you are free to go back to your hotel room for the rest of the day.

For those who don't feel safe off *piste* and who can't get up early, there's always the lunch hour. Aim to get up the mountain just as the others come in to eat and then head straight out saying you like the uncrowded slopes. Be careful, however, about where you go. Many mountain restaurants are situated to provide a view of the more spectacular *pistes*. Avoid these areas at all costs.

It is clear that Avoidance Skiing, at least in its purer forms, does presuppose a certain level of ability, particularly to get about in off *piste* areas. And however attractive the idea, especially if you can find some convivial hostelries to do your avoiding in (one reason, by the way, that Brits often confuse off *piste* with off pissed), it may be wise to be a bit less ambitious.

10. Skiing à l'Anglaise

**'In spite of their hats being terribly ugly, God damn! I love
the English'**

Pierre Jean De Béranger

Considering that Britain invented modern downhill skiing (that's our story) and produced many of the great Alpinists (the names of Whymper and Roberts of Kandahar are not forgotten in the Alps) it might be said that the British have let things slide a bit since. Not a bit of it. It's true that since those early days when only the British were racing downhill other nations have come to dominate championship skiing. But this has now developed into a rather crude form of the art, flashily commercial, with all the subtlety of old sacrificed to speed, and where the only important thing seems to be winning. The Englishman instead has chosen to stay aloof, remaining true to his amateur tradition and making his contribution on the holiday slopes. It is here that he has continued to excel, foregoing the glamour of the World Cup perhaps, but contributing mightily to that range of Survival Skiing know-how that the package deal *piste* basher depends on.

Much has been said of the advances made by Killy, Thoeni and Stenmark, but not enough, surely, of the achievements of Watkins, Thomas, Smith and others. Yet these are the men who, with their inventiveness and determination, have made the more important breakthroughs, forging the techniques which enable the fortnight-a-year man to keep his end up.

Perhaps one day, when someone adds up all the trophies, badges and diplomas won in ski-school end-of-week races, the immense contribution of these unsung heroes will be recognised.

In some respects, in fact, it is the Stenmarks of this world who have been shown the way by the Smiths. It is only fairly recently, for instance, that the speed merchants have learnt the lesson that the big races are won not on the steep bits but by how well the flatter parts are negotiated. However, an appreciation of the importance of the flat has long been conventional wisdom among the Smiths. Indeed, it is on the flat that you will most often find the Smiths working and practising their technique.

Much of what is said about the Smiths, of course, applies to Survival Skiers in general. Nevertheless, there's no question that the British do stand out from the rest and that one can legitimately talk about a clearly recognisable *style Anglais*. Let's try therefore to analyse this style in more detail. These are the main postural characteristics:

a)   *Absence of forward lean*. The British skier tends to stay fairly erect.

b)   *Bottom sticking out.* Believed to add stability.
c)   *Fiercely rotating shoulders.* Gets a bit of movement into the action.
d)   *Stiff lower leg.* Particularly on steep bits or moguls. Shows character, too.
e)   *Loose lower lip.* Ideal for recounting experiences at the bar.
f)   *Tendency to wave sticks about.* Helps to add interest to the action.
g)   *Intermittent rhythmical swaying.* Invariably after refreshment stops and at the end of the day.

The British skier will usually be found on shortish skis, wearing a distinctive hat and with his sunglasses worn correctly over the eyes rather than on top of the head. His boots will be Italian and his anorak or knee-length cagoule (well waterproofed as he goes out in all weathers) will have extra large pockets for carrying *The Sunday Times Ski Book* around. He will certainly have a bum-bag, often on the large side, in which, being safety-conscious, he will keep things like crêpe bandages, a whistle and salt tablets. Somewhere about his person, St Bernard style, he will also have a brandy flask for those all too frequent emergencies.

Even in the old days the British set the sartorial tone on the slopes. You need only look at those Victorian photographs of gallant Englishwomen climbing in their long skirts and red flannel petticoats. For the very cold weather there were undergarments called 'toasties' and headpieces called 'snuglets'. An additional whiff of refinement came from the bamboo perfume sprayed on the mittens.

So it seems fair to say that the British have always stood out in the mountains. The mere title of Sir Arnold Lunn's anthology *The Englishman on Ski* (you went out on ski in the old days, not skis) makes clear that an Englishman in the Alps was in no way to be confused with a Frenchman in the Alps, or anyone else for that matter.

But the English skier has undoubtedly evolved considerably over the years. It began with the almost regal English 'milord'. He was followed by the gentleman tourist who sent letters to Lunn for his yearbook. Today the more distinctive types are chalet-dwelling Hooray Henrys with their Sloane Ranger molls and *piste* clogging package dealers with Union Jack hats and compact skis.

One thing has changed little, however. The British have always seen it as their role to try to *amuser les autres*. Perhaps it can be traced right back to when Colonel Napier set the whole of Davos laughing by arriving at the Grand Hotel with a Norwegian butler and two pairs of skis (quite a novelty at that time). The butler's party piece was to ski down the slopes near the hotel holding aloft a tray with a cup and saucer on it.

Another characteristic of the skiing Briton, from ski-running days to the present, has been his determination to go out in all weathers, and not to take the soft

options. Lunn, for instance, was highly contemptuous of the sort of 'Cresta skier who never climbs a yard if he can help it'. Today, too, the British continue to live up to their 'mad dogs and Englishmen' reputation, venturing out in the most atrocious conditions to do battle with the elements. Cynics might say that this is not just a matter of mere fortitude since, as most Brits only manage two weeks skiing a year and each day represents about a week's salary, they can't afford to miss out. A week's lift pass alone probably costs as much as an annual season ticket from London to Brighton. Anyway, Britons continue to be contemptuous of those continental 'fair weather' skiers who believe in taking the third day off to rest.

This attitude may also have something to do with the rugged traditions of Scottish skiing, an unsung heritage where Skiing Man is truly put to the test. This, you will hear Brits hold forth, is 'real' skiing, bearing little relation to that namby-pamby *piste* bashing on well-manicured slopes under bright blue Alpine skies. Just take your average *Pistenjaeger* and park him on Glenshee and you'd soon find out what he was really made of. Alternatively, perhaps, put him on one of the other skiing surfaces like mud, grass or water; that would be a test of his mettle. It takes a good man to outski a Brit on one of these surfaces.

Certainly, there are no apologies to be made for Scottish skiing. After all, the Scots had mountains when Switzerland was as flat as a bedboard. Don't forget to keep mentioning that the Alps are very 'young' mountains.

This does not mean to say that privately British skiers may not hope things turn out a little better for them during the next Ice Age. Either that or bring back the Empire so that skiing in the Saltoro Range of the Karakoram in the Himalayas would again be like skiing in one's own backyard.

Not that the height of mountains need necessarily have all that much to do with skiing pedigree. It can be pointed out that the day the first British skier strapped sticks to his feet and slid was as far back as Saxon times and that these modest beginnings are still celebrated every year at the feast of St Swooshius in the Somerset village of Steep where the locals dance about with burning brands tied to their feet. One theory has it that the practice was brought over by the Vikings. But there is also what looks like a Roman ski-jump at Bath, so it is possible that one can trace things back even further. There's no guarantee that anyone will believe this, of course, but there's no harm in trying.

In fact, the British skier is rather good at pointing things out and putting Continentals right on some of the more common misconceptions. When not cutting a dash on the slopes he will often be found performing with even greater distinction at the bar, offering his advice, his wind unchallenged. There's many a Champagne Charlie who can dominate a big hotel by his voice alone. Similarly no-one can take over a whole resort as effectively as a group of hard-drinking young Scots looking for some opposition in a 'boat race'.

And why not blow the trumpet a bit? There may have been a few Swiss resorts, like Gstaad, that the British didn't start, but not many. And just because a man can't stem christie, that's no reason to restrain him from talking about how his grandmother went up the Matterhorn with Whymper.

Ski-talk, like queuing, seems to suit the British. One reason may be that much of what's said is about the weather. Brits are also good at kindly enquiries about other people's welfare: 'Did you have a good day? Have any falls?'

The British are equally at home in more erudite conversations. They may have fewer active skiers than other countries, but they almost certainly have a higher percentage of experts and theorists. British skiers have made a contribution to ski lore and verbiage well out of proportion to their numbers.

Amongst themselves, British skiers have been known to indulge at times in somewhat crude xenophobia – like making rude remarks about the quality of the machinery in Italy and Spain and its probable ancestry. There is also a frequently expressed conviction that somehow the British skier is getting a bad deal and it mightn't be a bad idea if the Continentals moved aside and let the British organise things for a change.

One feature of most British ski-talk is a determination to take the whole business very seriously. This may be because, despite the illustrious skiing heritage we have outlined, British mass skiing is still in its infancy and is therefore still undertaken with the earnestness of the novice.

This may also account for the unflagging enthusiasm of most Brits; coming to skiing later in years they find they have an exciting lifetime challenge ahead of them. By contrast, people born within range of the Alps who have skied from the

Pleasures of Skiing

EQUIPMENT

Wearing ski-boots. Ideally they will pinch in at least three places, be tight enough to guarantee that your toenails drop off at the end of a week, and ensure that a layer of skin is removed every two days.

Wearing *après-ski* boots. A less acute sensation, but memorable nevertheless. As with ski boots, there is the pleasure of clumping along like an astronaut. And there's the added delight of giving your feet a sweat bath. Most *après-ski* boots are synthetic and it's not long before they get all nice and squelchy, especially in overheated hotels.

Carrying skis. This is particularly enjoyable while walking uphill. Instructors generally have a groove dug into their shoulder to make it easier.

Getting a poke in the groin with a sharp stick. The attacker will be one of those people who carry their ski poles parallel to the ground and pointing backwards.

Getting a bash on the head. Usually happens when someone in front of you carrying skis over his shoulder suddenly swings round to ask for a light.

Worrying. Generally about whether someone is going to walk off with your skis in the lunch-break or remove your newly-purchased Dream Boots from the ski-room overnight.

cradle can usually do everything perfectly by their teens and find it all rather a bore. They then have to go in for ballet or hot-dogging or something equally undignified to generate any interest.

Like the Americans, the British are equipment-minded and take a lot of pleasure in the mechanical side. They always have a lot of sensible points to make about things like edges and if there's repair work to be done on the slopes it's normally the Brit in the group who will produce the screwdriver. Unlike most Continentals, who don't touch their equipment from one year to the next, the British skier is likely to spend the other 50 weeks of the year cleaning and oiling his bindings and performing the necessary surgery on the rest of his gear.

Part of this safety-consciousness may be because the British feel that much more vulnerable on skis. If your chances of being injured are rather high, you are more likely to produce the sort of chap who goes to the ski injury seminar and who knows the avalanche drill backwards and who is always worrying about where the nearest first-aid booth is. Or it may be just another hangover from those early days when the original Alpine Brits were invalids and convalescents. There is also, of course, no forgetting Whymper's grave at Chamonix.

The Whymper tradition has lived on in other ways, too. Like him, his countrymen are not frightened to take a tumble now and then – if only to help *les autres* feel more at ease. Some of the Continentals, on the other hand, tend to stand on their dignity somewhat and make rather a fetish of not falling down.

Everything considered, the British skier is a good all-rounder and certainly has no need to apologise for his performance. On the contrary, he should not be afraid to sound off a bit about the British School. Remember that everything that was worth saying about skiing was said as far back as 1910 by Vivian Caulfeild in *How to Ski* – even though he may have been a bit contemptuous of British efforts on the slopes.

So next time someone asks you about the length of your skis, why not reply in feet and inches?

11. The Rest

'The instructor was grimacing and gesticulating at me. "Ski parall-el, ski parall-el, m'sieu." That was only the beginning of his tirade. When his oration, which was almost political in its vehemence, was over he ran over to me, picked me up, shook me and put me down again. He was certainly agile. I wish I knew what it was he wanted me to do. I felt very gauche. My knees quaked and from the position in which he had left me, I fell.'

S. P. B. Mais, British Ski Year Book 1949

Although familiarity and appreciation of the British approach may help boost your ego, it's a knowledge of the various Continental styles that are more likely to help the Survival Skier get through his day successfully.

This is particularly true for group skiers who must choose a style of tuition that suits them. *Skilehrers, moniteurs* and *maestri* differ considerably, and the pros and cons need to be weighed up carefully. An instructor who enjoys talking, for instance, may bore and confuse but does have the advantage that he doesn't make you do so much skiing. A *poseur* of an instructor may be very irritating but he is going to spend less time looking at you and finding fault.

Let's look therefore at the main national approaches. Very broadly there are two main groups – the Latins (Italians, Spaniards and French) and the Mittel-Europeans (Germans, Austrians and Swiss).

The Latins

The Latins, in general, seem prepared to accept that you should enjoy your skiing and are less inclined to throw the rule book at you. Italians and Spaniards in particular are inclined to favour the 'follow me' approach. They know that, in the end, it's mileage that counts and that the real reason they can ski better than you is because they've put in a couple of million miles on skis since the age of three. They accept that you are unlikely to understand, let alone absorb, anything much of what they say, so they don't waste too much time on explanations. That doesn't mean they don't spend time talking; they do, but it tends to be about the sunshine and the mountains and how they got on when they went over to London as a demonstrator at the *Daily Mail* Ski Show. They also manage to touch base at a fair number of refreshment stops in the course of a day and they don't mind too much if you decide to take rather more extended breaks or even slide off for the odd half day. After all, if they weren't getting paid for it, they'd do the same.

Pleasures of Skiing

MEMORABLE MOMENTS

When you realise you're heading for an Almighty Fall but haven't yet hit the ground.

When you get to an *omigod* precipice and realise that the only way to go is down. This moment is at its most poignant when you are holding up a lot of impatient people behind you.

When you try to put your skis back on in deep snow and keep trapping a thick wedge of snow between boot and binding. This is nearly as enjoyable as that pleasure from the past of lacing your binding cable under the lugs with freezing fingers after a fall.

When you get a boot or collar full of snow. Especially satisfying when the snow takes some while to melt.

When you lose your ski or ski-stick in deep snow. This can provide hours of fun and keep a whole class amused digging away.

When the instructor makes you spend the afternoon walking uphill on skis — especially when he makes you do it herringbone-style.

When you get shown up by an infant who's only been skiing for a matter of days — a constant pleasure since the slopes today are full of small people.

When it dawns on you that you'll probably never become quite as good as Jean-Claude Killy.

A disadvantage is their enthusiasm for departing from the straight and narrow. They often fail to perceive the class's reluctance to get involved with the *neve fresca*, or to get lost in the woods or to jump from patch of melting snow to patch of melting snow in order to ski right down to the village. (They are the ones who jump from patch to patch, of course — you just gouge out the bottom of your skis on the gravel in between.) Needless to say, all this considerably increases the possibility of casualties and people do from time to time get lost in crevasses and buried in drifts.

The French differ somewhat from the mainstream Latin approach. They also accept that skiing can be fun, but they are a lot more intellectual about it. Big talkers, they spend time explaining their personal philosophy of the art, and very often try to inflict upon you *avant-garde* techniques dreamed up by some Grenoble professor. Provided, however, you pay lip-service to the notion that

French skiing is where it's at and that there'll never be anyone else on *planches* quite like Killy, they can be reasonably pleasant to you.

A general point about the Latin group is that, on the whole, they are much better ego-boosters. At the end of your week, for instance, they will dole out all manner of ribbons and trinkets and certificates to make you feel good.

The Mittel-Europeans

The Mittel-European group reject the lighter Latin approach. Their view is that you're not there to enjoy yourself, you're there to ski; and skiing is something to be taken seriously — it is, after all, their livelihood. Skiing is good for you, but like many things that are supposed to be good for you, it is not necessarily enjoyable. It will be made clear from the start that the Austrians and the Swiss are the real skiing nations, and that you should forget any of the half-baked notions and sloppy ideas you may have picked up on the southern side of the Alps. There is only one way to ski — the proper way, the *Skitechnik* way, the way painstakingly evolved in the German-speaking Alps and codified in one of the definitive texts like the official Austrian manual for *staatlich geprüfte Skilehrer*.

The British, in general, seem to prefer this second approach to skiing. This may seem like sheer masochism but there are certain advantages to it. The instructors' long-winded lectures and technical explanations take up most of the time which means you can get by with less actual skiing. And their taste for bizarre exercises, often without sticks, also means you have to perform less. This is because each exercise takes time to explain and they are usually performed by the group one by one. Above all, Mittel-Europeans are sensible — no adventures — so your chances of ending the day in reasonable physical shape are fair. They also take a little more interest in the class and less in their own performance.

But one or two distinctions should be made between the different types of Mittel-European.

THE GERMANS

The Germans are very much the junior partners and don't really lay claim to their own national style. They will usually defer to the others as keepers of the skiing covenant. Their main distinguishing feature is an insistence on over-vigorous warm-up callisthenics, though this is compensated for by plenty of time-wasting concentration on safety drill and correct preparation and adjustment of equipment.

THE AUSTRIANS

The Austrians, like the French, need constant reassurance that they are the Tops when it comes to skiing. Their instructors are less intellectual but equally boring, as they repeat their litanies from the *Ski Instructors' Manual*. Sometimes the class is obliged to chant these litanies in unison — possibly while performing a manoeuvre. But if you are good at remembering what you are told, even if not necessarily doing what you are told, you can usually get off lightly.

THE SWISS

The Swiss have less of a complex about the whole thing — they know they are the Number One skiing nation. They, too, want it all to be done according to the

book but they probably don't take it out on you so much. Not on your body anyway; they do, however, hit you where it hurts most — in the wallet.

There are also, of course, the Scandinavians (principally the Norwegians) and the Americans — both of whom adopt a lower key, friendlier approach; 'skiing with a human face' as it's been called. The Scandinavians go on about it a lot less than the other nations, possibly because they don't take downhill skiing quite so seriously. For them *langlauf* is the real thing. American instructors, however, can get rather carried away. They are often excessively technical, can be almost as incomprehensible as the Continentals, are obsessed with new equipment and have a tendency to go on about the Ultimate Experiences they have had or hope to have. But for all that they do try to treat you as a human being and don't push you around too much (except when the instructor is playing Coach and telling you to 'Go For It').

It will be clear from this that ski-slopes are very fertile ground for national chauvinism. Every nation, for instance, lays claim to having invented the sport. The British know it was Henry Lunn who really started the Alpine thing off by organising that first package tour to a religious conference (convened by him) at Grindelwald in 1892; and anyway miners in the Cumberland fells were already using a form of ski back in the nineteenth century. The Austrians will tell you that their peasants were skiing in the province of Krain as early as the seventeenth century. The Swiss know that they are regarded by the world at large as the skiing nation *par excellence*. The Scandinavians point out that before anything got going in the Alps it was all happening in their neck of the woods and that they've got the cave paintings and the 2500 BC Hoting ski to prove it; even the 'modern' era was kicked off by Sondre Norheim at Christiania in 1866. The Italians and the French knock all these claims down by referring to ancient Chinese and tundra skiers and then go on about defunct sects of mediaeval skiing monks in the Jura or the Dolomites. The Americans will point out that it was Snow-shoe Thompson who, in the 1850's, was the first to find a practical application for skis.

As to which is the main skiing nation, the Italians will invite you to look at the map and see which country contains the biggest slice of the Alps. The French, instead, will invite you to study the modern ski era and look at which nation has been responsible for most of the research, innovations and major developments over the past 30 years.

The British do not rise above these controversies. They feel their role is to evaluate the competing claims and to arbitrate on some of the great doctrinal schisms such as 'open pole plant' versus 'closed pole plant'. They don't hesitate to put the other nations right on particular issues.

The British have also started to clean up some of the confusing foreign vocabulary. Tidied-up stem christies, for instance, have now become basic swing. This is rather a pity, in fact, because much of the magic comes from the foreign terminology. It all sounds so much better when you don't understand what it means. We all know that there are basically just two kinds of turn – one to the left and one to the right – but it makes you feel so much better if you can talk about *'ski aval'*, *'ski amont'* and *'projection circulaire'*.

For those who just don't like foreign words, it should be pointed out that the worst fate of all for a ski-class is to have an instructor of the same nationality. There is then no excuse for incomprehension and the class has no opportunity to indulge in the collective xenophobia towards the instructor which is part of the fun.

What usually happens in single nationality groups is that the instructor spends much of his time leading the class in making catty remarks about the skiing prowess of some of the other nationalities represented *en piste*. There's an awful smugness about English, Dutch, Danish, German or American groups who take their own man along – a growing trend among these nationalities. Their line tends to be that other countries may ski better, but they can teach better. As a result you are subjected to the most boring monologues of the lot – and there's not even any escape in the evening as the chap will be in the same hotel as you.

12. Skiing Types

'It is in the ability to deceive oneself that the greatest talent is shown'

Anatole France

In addition to being aware of the different national approaches to skiing, the well-prepared Survival Skier should also be able to identify the more common individual types on the slopes – most of which cut across national lines. The following are sketches of some who stand out. (Even though, for convenience, only the masculine pronoun is used, it should not be imagined that they are confined to one sex.)

THE MEASURER

Obsessed with ski lengths and talks of little else. Usually strikes in queues where skis are being carried. He stands his skis alongside yours and asks: 'What are they – 180s?' He then proceeds to tell you how he was on 175s, is now on 185s but is thinking of eventually settling on 190s.

THE SURGEON

Spends most of his time waxing and sharpening and adjusting bindings. When on the slopes can't wait for someone's skis to break down so he can show off his collection of screwdrivers. Always on the lookout for snow conditions that severely damage skis so as to make his evening surgery sessions more interesting and challenging.

THE SUN-WORSHIPPER

Usually to be found sitting, standing or lying down – almost never skiing. Face is always turned to the sun, eyes closed. Only interrupts this to apply new layer of sun cream.

THE NON-IMPROVER

Can't work out why he is in a lower class this year than he was last year and why he's now being forced by the instructor to learn things he had taped years ago. He's constantly referring back to some mythical time when his skiing was sheer poetry and the instructor thought he had real potential.

THE ADVISER

Can't ski but makes up for it by omniscience. Usually lets the instructor say his bit, then comes in with the definitive interpretation of why you cocked it up. The most amusing thing is watching him try to demonstrate: 'Well, it's not quite like that, but you know what I mean.'

THE T-BAR ADVISER

A very close relative who's no more competent on the T-bar than the other is at skiing. Normally seeks out novices to go up with. If you do have the misfortune to join him, he'll spend all his time explaining about T-bar technique and what you're doing wrong. 'Relax,' he'll say, convinced that the fact that you're both about to fall off is your fault rather than his.

THE PANTHEIST

Often German or Scandinavian. In love with nature, always gazing at the mountains, taking deep breaths or smiling into the sun. When people pass he beams and sighs 'Herrlich' or 'Spitze, nicht?'

THE SNOW BUFF

Usually found cupping snowflakes in hand and explaining to anyone who's prepared to listen that there are literally thousands of different types of them, and that the Eskimos have a word for just about every one. Carries small books in his bum-bag to help him identify different formations of snow crystal.

THE METEOROLOGIST

Much akin to the snow buff but more doom-laden and less entranced by the magic of the mountains. Usually occupied scanning the horizon and predicting changing weather conditions. Also has plenty to say about snow surfaces, potential avalanches and hidden crevasses.

THE SAFETY NUT

Spends most of his money on the latest bindings and spends most of his time adjusting them. Knows the drill for all emergency situations and usually sports a number of first-aid badges. His bum-bag, of course, is well stocked with medical, and even surgical, bits and pieces. Off the slopes he's usually busy attending a ski injury seminar or going to the map-reading class.

THE HAPPY WANDERER

Sets off in the morning armed with *Alpenstock* or *piolet* and returns in the evening laden with mountain flowers. Rightly contemptuous of your activities.

THE TALL STORY-TELLER

Always on about the mogul that got away and the time he came down the Devil's Elbow on only one ski or how he'd done five runs by the time you arrived on the slopes at nine o'clock.

THE MACHINERY MARVELLER

Often accompanied by children on whom he inflicts his worship of snowcats, ski-lifts, cable cars and all the other mechanical contrivances on the slopes. Never tires in his wonder and faith in these machines. Two words that would never occur to him are 'metal fatigue'.

THE HUMAN AVALANCHE

Fancies himself as a bit of a 'bomber'. Specialises in skiing beyond the limit of his generally modest talents. Perpetually covered in snow, he wastes little time picking himself up from his crashes and hurtles straight on to the next disaster.

THE CLASS FOULER-UPPER

A cousin of the human avalanche. Can always be counted on to see that no group effort goes off as it should. If, for instance, the line is peeling off from top to bottom, he'll break ranks to make sure that the order is not followed. When skiing down to the class he will invariably try to join at the top, or, if he misses his last turn, somewhere in the middle, usually managing to knock everybody down.

THE JOKER

Another relative. Enjoys standing on the back of your skis, flicking snow at you with his ski-sticks, throwing snowballs and similar activities. Also has a limited range of 'silly positions' which he keeps inviting you to watch him perform.

THE *SKI ÉVOLUTIF* FANATIC

Usually has children. Had the whole family on *ski évolutif* in France once and has never got over the discovery. Spends a lot of time in obscure resorts in places like Bulgaria, demanding to know why they don't offer *ski évolutif* or why they've never even heard of it.

THE PHOTOGRAPHER

Identifiable by his huge black bag which he will sometimes manage to get the instructor to carry for him. Amiable enough, but keeps the class hanging around a lot while he sets up the equipment – especially if it's cine. Most irritating trick is to make the class walk uphill in deep powder snow so he's got the right background for his picture.

THE LINGUIST

Has a smattering of the instructor's tongue and so volunteers to translate for the rest of the class. In fact he misses most of what's said, but as he usually feels he knows a bit about skiing himself, he'll prattle on, inflicting his own half-baked theories on the rest of the class.

THE POWDER FREAK

Is always going on about *la poudreuse* or *neve fresca* or *Pulverschnee*. He knows the name for it in most languages. Spends a lot of *en piste* time sitting back, with sticks out, imitating the motions for powder skiing. Is usually a lot less successful when he actually gets into the stuff but is always whining at the instructor anyway to take the class off *piste*.

THE IMBIBER/NIBBLER

Keeps the day well punctuated with refreshment stops at friendly hostelries, fortifying drams on the slopes or smoke breaks. Always has a flask of alcohol about his person and probably some *saucisson*, nuts and chocolate, too. Worth keeping in with.

THE EARLY BIRD

Has faded gear and old fashioned equipment and always arrives back in the ski-room just as you are setting out of a morning. Makes a point of telling everyone very heartily how there's nothing like 'first run'. This person may just be a skilful Survival Skier, but it's probably not worth getting up early to find out.

THE ACCUSER

Always has someone or something to blame for his difficulties. Either you were skiing on his tail or he couldn't follow the funny line you took. The snow always seems to organise itself just to thwart his efforts.

THE *PISTENJAEGER*

The smoothie who knows how to ski. Is actually rather bored with skiing but enjoys being admired, envied, hated, and so keeps at it. Usually performs on difficult bits that are in full view of lots of people (e.g. on 'Watch Me' mogulfields). Very helpful to attractive beginners of the opposite sex. The more flamboyant types have taken to wearing a silk handkerchief knotted around the thigh.

THE VETERAN

Has been returning to the same hotel in the same resort for the past few decades and always occupies his particular corner of the hotel bar or nearby *Stübli* where he has his own personal beer *Stein*. Spends his time there mumbling to the barman about the snows of yesteryear and the *Thé Dansants* of yore and the good old days when people went ski-touring, dressed for dinner and had intelligent discourse on the respective merits of using one, two or no sticks.

THE SKI NEUROTIC

Increasingly common. Constantly worrying about whether he's on the right type of skis, or whether he hasn't perhaps got worse since last year. Always goes to the instructor after class to ask if he might be better off having private lessons geared to his particular needs. More and more shrinks are going into full-time ski psychiatry to cater for this new breed of patient, and many instructors are on commission for referring patients to them. (Slogan in the consulting room of one Californian nut doctor: 'First get your head together, then get your feet together'.)

THE ZEN SKIER

A close cousin of the ski neurotic. Invariably American. He's usually wearing a headband, carrying a copy of *Inner Skiing* and chanting a mantra. In action, adopts funny positions to 'listen to the sound of his skis' or to concentrate on some other specific part of his anatomy. When not on the slopes he can be found doing yoga somewhere in the hotel.

THE 'ULTIMATE' FREAK

Another relative. Also usually American. He's on an unending search for the 'ultimate' ski experience; or failing that, anything he can say 'Wow', 'Holy Shit' or 'Hit me' about while he's waiting. If there's no helicopter skiing, he'll be off *piste* somewhere in unskied powder. Usually manages to find new and highly dangerous routes down, preferably involving a bit of jumping, during which he will yip at the top of his voice. He's also embarrassingly enthusiastic about equipment. All his gear is either handcrafted or the 'ultimate' product of the latest space age technology. He is, of course, already planning to trade it in as new stuff is about to appear on the market that is even more 'ultimate'. He will also be the proud possessor of a mono-ski so if you want to shake him off the simplest thing is just to go up the Poma-lift — unless, of course, he happens to be bow-legged.

THE CHALET DWELLERS

Several varieties of these. Often British. One lot are very hearty with piercing South Ken voices. They spend a lot of time swapping names of people they have in common, eating fondues and forgetting to do the washing-up. A second lot are a bit more down-market and keep talking about how they enjoy 'mucking in together'. They are always arguing about whose turn it is to do the washing-up or use the bathroom first and live on instant soup and baked beans from the local supermarket. Both groups easily drown out a third lot — the guitar-players and songsters. These people don't wash much (the others don't give them much chance) and don't wash up because they live on bread, cheese and wine.

THE PROUD PARENTS

Do their skiing through their children. First enrolled Jason with DHO when he was three and he's now in the West Norfolk under-fives slalom team. They're thinking of coming to live permanently in Switzerland. Meanwhile they travel out to the Alps every other month in a battered mini-bus plastered with ski stickers. They often team up with similar families for these trips so that the fathers can play at being team managers. The big advantage for the parents is that they feel involved in the Big Time but don't actually have to do much skiing. Their biggest gripe is that no firm has yet been prepared to sponsor their offspring: 'No wonder we can't keep up with the East Germans'.

THE SHOPPER

Spends most of his time going round the shops, trying things on and even studying items already bought on previous days. Is never sure whether things are cheaper at home or on the mountain. He only goes out on the slopes to test or show off his latest acquisition. This will always be pointed out to you for admiration, envy or approval; if it wasn't pointed out you'd never know it was new as he doesn't have a single item of gear that's old.

THE RESORT COLLECTOR

Doesn't do much skiing but claims to have skied an awful lot. You name it, he's been there – done all the right things. If it's St Moritz then his hangouts will have been the Palace Bar, the Corviglia Club and Hanselmanns. He must either spend half his life travelling or an awful lot of time studying brochures.

THE PRIVATE LESSON TAKERS

Usually a couple. They can't take the abuse in bigger classes and feel that they have latent skiing talent (usually very latent indeed) that could be brought out by a more personal form of tuition. Their instructor knows what he's being paid for and does his bit at making them feel a lot better than they are. They spend the evenings telling each other and everyone else how the lessons are worth every penny and what tremendous progress they are making.

THE REPORTER

Occupies himself by feeding you snippets of information about what's going on in the outside world, never imagining for a moment that the reason you're on the mountain is to sever all connection with the outside world. He's usually armed with a pocket transistor radio capable of picking up the moon and he gets his written information by hanging around at the newsagent's scanning the front page headlines with the aid of a selection of pocket dictionaries.

13. Après-Ski

'Rise up lads, the evening is coming . . .'

Catullus

Strictly speaking, *après-ski* refers to those other winter sports, like ice-skating, curling, or sleigh-riding, that you go in for when you come off the slopes. Everyone knows, though, that what it really means is putting on a chunky sweater and lounging around on a bearskin rug in front of a blazing log fire with one arm round a jug of *Glühwein* and the other round an attractive companion.

The trouble is that this cosy picture of skiers who came in from the cold (which may have lured us into the mountains in the first place) is not really true either. In fact, *après-ski* is more like a nightly social assault course which can take more out of you than your on-slope activities. Don't be misled into thinking *après-ski* is the easy part. If anything, it's the skiing that's got easier over the years (yes really), while the *après-ski* has got tougher.

The real problem is that *après-ski* and skiing don't go together. Skiing doesn't leave you in much shape for *après-ski* and vice versa. Night-time knees-ups and daytime knees-bends are not all that compatible. But you paid for both. You *will* enjoy both.

The good thing about *après-ski* is that you are not at the same disadvantage vis-a-vis the pros as you are on the slopes. We all have plenty of opportunity during the rest of the year to practise getting drunk, sing-songing, disco-dancing or whatever form of carousing happens to be our forte. Indeed, there are plenty of rotten skiers who are in the front rank of *après-skiers*, and it's probably true to say that among the all-time great *après-skiers* very few have been any good on the ski-slopes.

Many of the big names on the ski-circuit avoid *après-ski* altogether. But don't let any of the ski-nuts on your holiday do the same. If a keen *après-skier* like you does his bit on the slopes, there's no reason why the skiers should cop out of the bar sessions. If you are prepared to be shown up during the day, they should be prepared to be shown up at night. *Après-skiers* therefore make it their business to see that skiers don't sneak off to bed early and skimp on the *après-ski*.

If some people do insist on jacking out of the *Gemütlichkeit* (couples are the worst offenders) it's unlikely to do them much good. *Après-skiers* can usually make enough noise in every corner of a resort to ensure that nobody gets to sleep before they do.

The fact that skiing and *après-skiing* don't always marry up too well doesn't mean that skiing techniques don't come into *après-ski*. As on the slopes, a lot of time is spent posing and there's probably more ski-talking *après-ski* than during ski.

Stand back some time and watch a group of skiers standing at a bar. They'll all be bending right or left in banana position, weight on the lower foot, pushing their knees forward as they make a point and leaning into the bar as if it was the Fall Line. Similar postures can be seen at the disco. Everyone will be weighting and unweighting as they roll their knees and bump bottoms (a favourite with skiers who tend to have quite large ones).

Although this is all quite unconscious, there is also a good deal of deliberate demonstrating. Many people find it easier to execute certain manoeuvres at the bar than on the slopes, and even quite undistinguished skiers seem to feel they can pull off some of the more exotic turns very successfully when legless. But do resist any temptation to rush down to get your skis and show people how to do it on the stairs. It's more difficult than it is on snow and the landlord won't like it.

The *après-ski* begins as soon as you arrive back in the ski-room where you show off your best bruises and have a preliminary undress rehearsal for your stories of the day's escapades. The exercise continues over some form of hot grog at your *Stammtisch* in the local *Weinstube*, enabling you to further restore your circulation and your ego. This usually ends in a bit of a scramble as people make a dash for their rooms to try to get to the hot water while there's still some left.

These days it's more the thing, particularly if you're a top-floor dweller who didn't make it in time, to do your bathing in public — at the swimming pool and sauna. Exposure to heat can seem like quite a good idea after a day of exposure to cold. Those who've had enough exposure for one day stay at the poolside draped in their towelling robes and continue drinking. There's usually a bar attached or one within staggering distance. Some people even swim. For a change of scene you can always go and play with the apparatus in the gymnasium or solarium.

But the real *après-skiers* take a sauna and a massage, proclaiming heartily that dehydration and pummelling are good for you after a day on the slopes. The sauna can be fun. Most of them are mixed now and the regulars can have hours of harmless pleasure steaming it up or turning up the thermostat to drive out the novices.

You need not be deprived of the comfort of alcohol as you sweat it out. The sauna hour can, in fact, turn into a very heavy session – especially if there are Scandinavians about. They usually insist on bringing large quantities of beer and aquavit inside for instant replacement of lost liquid. If you get round to chucking beer instead of water on the stones it makes for an even headier atmosphere.

Some people can get quite carried away in the sauna – again, usually Scandinavians or Germans. Instead of lying there semi-conscious reading a newspaper and getting drunk, they keep dashing out to roll in the snow, jump into an ice-cold lake if there's one handy or, failing that, the plunge pool. They also beat each other with rolled up newspapers or flick each other with towels, presumably as a substitute for birch twigs. If the going gets too rough, retire to the solarium to work on your suntan.

After all, the bathing hour is supposed to be for the less sporty individuals. The real athletes will be outside again for another bout of hard physical exercise – ice-skating, bowling, or sometimes jogging despite the obvious difficulties in a ski resort. Some even head back out to the *pistes* – a lot of places now have floodlit lower slopes. But a word of warning to Survival Skiers: these slopes are always prominently situated to provide entertainment for more sensible people sitting and drinking inside.

The next item in the *après-skiing* programme is usually shopping. This is perhaps the most relaxing pre-dinner activity, most skiers have a strong urge to spend money which will have been largely frustrated on the slopes during the day. It's also a good morale-booster as shopping is something most people know how to do.

The shopping stroll is often combined with a stoking-up-before-dinner session, which means dropping into one of the many pastry and ice-shops and exercising your jaws and your waistband on some *Strudel*, *gâteau* or *cassata*. Another alternative in the old days used to be the *Thé Dansant*, which seems to have been phased out at even the poshest resorts, though there are attempts in some hotels to replace it with an American-style Happy Hour.

After this people are usually ready for dinner, which takes place early in ski resorts. Skiers, even Survival Skiers, are always hungry and eat a lot.

People no longer dress for dinner – except in their *après-ski* suits – and no longer seem to feel it's not the done thing to be among the first into the dining room. In fact, people tend to gather at the bar and charge in as soon as the dining

room doors open. It does, of course, pay to start early if you're somewhere like Switzerland and may be put to work on the slow business of cooking your own in a fondue pot.

Make the most of dinner. Linger over your myrtle tart or your *crêpe*. As soon as it's over there'll be little chance to escape from the action.

Some of the ski-freaks, of course, now go back to those floodlit slopes yet again. But most people will choose to do their sliding to and from the *Weinstube*, night-club or disco.

It is on these little expeditions to and from your local hotspot — usually from —

that most skiing accidents occur. Clearly you've quite a good chance of breaking your leg on some slippery path wearing your non-grip *après-ski* boots, slightly the worse for alcohol poisoning, being pelted with snowballs and writhing about when someone puts snow down your back.

It is after dinner that you sort out the real *après-skiers*. Those who can't handle it will opt for some tame diversion like sitting around playing cards or draughts or watching films with titles like 'White Dreams' of people hot-dogging or floating in slow motion through the powder. Ski-tourers will sit studying their maps and would-be racers will go and sharpen and wax their boards.

The true *après-skiers* will be down at the *Weinstube*, beer-on-draught 'English pub' or *Bierkeller* already linking arms and getting stuck in to their *Schunkellieder*. These usually turn into national team affairs — the Germans with their oompah songs, the Italians hitting the higher notes and trying something a bit more melodic like *O Sole Mio* and the British confusing the opposition with *On Ilkley Moor Bah't 'at*.

You may well be joined at the *Weinstube* by your ski instructor. Try not to let him upset your drinking as much as he does your skiing. He'll probably encourage you to try the local firewater, but there's no point in letting him choose the weapons all the time. He was probably weaned on this stuff.

Be equally cautious about getting involved in other local customs like *Schuhplatter* dancing, balancing on beer *Steins*, yodelling, alpenhorn-blowing or skiing down flights of stairs. However much the instructor or dirndl-clad maid may enjoin you to '*sei nicht so feig*', these are offers you definitely can refuse. Stick with things you know how to do — like limbo-dancing or swinging from the chandeliers. But don't imagine you'll be on home ground if you move over to the dart board — if it's been there at least six months the chances are the locals will be more accurate with the arrows than you are.

If you do decide to perform any of your favourite party tricks, it's as well to remember that it can be more difficult after eight hours on the snow and one in the sweat-box. Your body may feel you've asked enough of it for one day.

You may be better off linking arms with your neighbour (one advantage of *après-skiing* over skiing is that you can use other people to hold yourself up) swaying to the music and watching some foolhardy innocent take on the alpenhorn.

Before you are too far gone you'll have to make a move and stagger on to the last stage of the evening's *après-ski*. This could be the casino or a bout of serious drinking in some murky cellar or, more probably, hopping about in *Pferdestall*, night-club or disco. The first two are likely to be the hardest — one on your pocket and one on your liver. The night spots are the most popular choice, provided you think you've still got the legs for it. It's also an opportunity to come alongside

Skiing Statistics

Most people ski between 40– 70 per cent better in their mind's eye than they do on the slopes.

The stranger you gave advice to in the bar will turn out the next day to be twice as good as you are.

You are three times more likely to break your leg going down the path to the disco or going downstairs in the restaurant in your ski-boots than you are while skiing.

Your lift pass will cost at least 150 per cent more than you thought it would.

At 2,000 metres a three and a half minute egg needs to be boiled for six minutes.

Your teeth are four times more likely to ache at altitude.

whoever it is you've been lusting after on the slopes – if you can recognise him or her out of their ski-gear, that is.

If you don't go with a partner, it's certainly a good idea to lose no time in seeking one out. It's vital to have someone to lean on on the dance floor and to help you keep your head above table level.

The more experienced *après-skiers* should also try to keep their eyes open for any of the weaker bretheren who try to slip off to bed, perhaps claiming that they've got to adjust their bindings for the morrow. One way of stopping this is to pool all the room keys. People don't normally like to be the first to draw a strange bed and an unfamiliar bedfellow unless it's a proper key-swapping party night.

One of the main things to remember on this last stage – particularly on the journey back – is to keep the noise level up. No-one in the resort should be allowed to get to sleep before you do. Just to make sure, one of your number is usually detailed to go and knock on all the other bedroom doors before going to bed. Strictly speaking this shouldn't happen much before 3 am, otherwise those already in bed will conclude that you haven't really enjoyed yourself.

If you are sharing an apartment or a room with someone who has already got their head down, make sure you turn on all the lights, make a fair old racket and ask them (several times, if necessary) if they are asleep. They also often appreciate it if you open the window wide for a refreshing blast of cold air. Remember, he who goes to bed last sleeps best.

You will sometimes come across people who don't take this in the proper spirit and, rather childishly, try to take revenge by tipping you out of bed in the early morning. This need not worry you too much since, if they don't tip you out, the chalet or hotel maid certainly will. These good people (who have the sense not to sleep on the premises) are totally unfamiliar with the concept of the lie-in and are under orders to see that all visitors are dispatched to the ski-slopes during the day.

This is one reason why it's best not to pass too often that point in the small hours when *après-skiing* more or less turns into *avant-skiing* and it no longer seems worth the effort of taking your boots off.

Nevertheless the real stayers will often remain active a while longer groping under the sheets – doing their best to keep those promises made on the disco floor. Some hold that an early morning grope is a good way of loosening up for the day ahead. Ski instructors say it can give you the idea of the sort of rhythm you should be looking for in your parallels. But it seems fair to say you may not notice much immediate improvement on the slopes the next day.

14. The Natives

'Those rascals of the mountains who practise every kind of cruelty imaginable on travellers'

Michel De Montaigne

If you ever get lost or stuck somewhere in the mountains, whether it's a precipitous by-road or a darkening ski-slope, the odds are that sooner or later you will find yourself face to face with some canny old Mountain Man who knows you are his victim. This is the native in his purest form. His forefathers made a killing whenever Hannibal and Napoleon came the way of the Alps. And now you are going to help him to get through the winter by letting him help you – at a price, of course – to find food, shelter, petrol, a mechanic, the way down or whatever else it is you need.

This man is a member of the same clan – albeit one of the wilder cousins – as those who staff the ski resort of your choice and fleece you in today's more organised and sophisticated way. They no longer have to lie in wait for travellers. They've spun a web of *pistes* and ski-lifts over the mountain and baited it with goodies to lure you up to 1500 metres for your two week spending spree.

It's important not to delude yourself about this. For, as a keen skier who has spent the rest of the year yearning for the clean air and the open sky of the high ground, you may feel yourself to be something of an Honorary Mountain Man or Woman yourself. That may be the way you feel. But to the real mountain folk the word skier means only one thing – tourist.

The appearance of the first ski-runners raring to get at the snow must have seemed like an answer to one of the eternal mysteries. For thousands of years mountain folk must have asked themselves what the point was of the snows that came every year to drive them with their livestock into winter hibernation. They've since found out. Now they know that the snow is their most precious resource, and renewable annually to boot. Their only regret is that they didn't start showing the lowlanders how to strap barrel staves to their feet earlier.

Just how slow they were on the uptake can be gauged from the fact that, as late as the end of the last century, a family in the ice-cream business in Granada in Southern Spain had no difficulty in acquiring rights to the exclusive use of all the snow on the Sierra Nevada for their trade. These rights, incidentally, have been handed down through the family until today, but they've been decent enough to let people ski on the snow and so enable the local ski industry to flourish. They put the title up for sale every now and then; so if anyone's looking for an exotic present for the girl who has everything . . .

It probably won't be long, in fact, before the whole business of snowing – that quirk of nature on which Mountain Man has come to depend – will be taken out of the hands of the Gods. Snow-making machines can only go on getting better and we will soon have the technology for inducing the right temperatures over the tops of mountains to precipitate the stuff.

Certainly Mountain Man has not been slow to take advantage of and adapt to whatever mechanical paraphenalia lowland man can dream up. It's hard to believe sometimes, looking at the complex complex of a modern ski resort, that what is being offered are still the basics of food, shelter and mountain know-how.

It must be especially hard to believe for the locals, who probably spend a lot of time pinching themselves and wondering for how much longer the goose is going to lay his golden eggs. Is it possible that these lowland masochists are still going to want to come all that way to be abused by the locals on the slopes? Can there be enough money left down there for people to continue to be able to hand over such huge sums for the privilege of going up and down on sundry mechanical contrivances in conditions that no self-respecting brass monkey would be out in? Will young lowland men with PhDs continue to want to throw it all up to become ski bums?

The locals themselves are not sure exactly what the magic formula is that keeps these people coming to spend their money in remote and inhospitable places. But they do by now have a fairly good idea of some of the basic ingredients they have to provide.

One of the most important of these is the setting. Ideally there should be an important mountain in the area to serve as a backdrop and, of course, to feature on most of the local picture postcards. Other outstanding climatic or geographical features – like a glacier or a special type of wind (*Foehn*, for instance) – also help.

When it comes to the slopes, it is usual to have a *piste* or a piece of *piste* apparatus that can claim to be the 'mostest'. Thus you might have the longest *piste*, or the widest, or the one with the biggest camber, or with the most moguls, or with the biggest vertical drop. The lift could be the longest T-bar, the T-bar with the most bends or the fastest running T-bar. Competition between resorts being what it is, many villages are obliged to qualify these claims, so you often get something like 'the longest Poma-lift on an east-facing slope in the Romansch-speaking Alps'.

Each village has a statistician who collects all this data and collates it with the latest statistics from other resorts, so as to lend a specious authority to the claims that are made.

Most resorts also have a fellow whose job it is to think up names for newly-opened slopes, *pistes*, lifts and mountain restaurants. The Americans have a particular talent for this, inventing names like 'Don't look now', 'My God', 'Watch me' and 'Never again'.

These two individuals work very closely with another important character – the local Pathological Liar. He's the one who rings up the national newspapers with the snow reports and who persuades the National Ski Club representatives that it really is possible, or very shortly will be, to ski on the Neverneve.

This last job is often held in rotation by different people in the village, since the incumbent fairly rapidly becomes discredited. Most of the locals can do the job as nearly all Mountain Men think of themselves as amateur meteorologists. It's a role that is certainly expected of them by their guests. In answer to a question about what the weather is likely to do, they can all be counted upon to turn out a first-rate performance. They'll narrow the eyes, look up, scan the horizon, sniff the air, taste it, put a finger up for the wind, scoop up a little snow, eat it and then come up with something suitably Delphic that you can interpret as you wish. Sometimes they'll offer up a more specific piece of local weather lore like 'When the wind is in the East it's neither fit for man nor beast' or 'It always snows on the fifteenth night of the year when the moon is new and the birds are flying west in threes'.

At best this will be enacted by a wizened, red-nosed, wind-tanned, bow-legged old Mountain Man, complete with pipe and stick. These old fellows used to provide some of the best examples of local colour. Unfortunately, because of the softer life in the mountains in recent years, there are fewer authentic specimens around these days. As a result an Alpine version of Central Casting has been set up and is doing excellent business providing suitably gnarled freelancers who do the rounds of the villages and pose for photographers.

Rather more likely to feature on your picture postcards are local girls and boys in folksy costume, perhaps *Dirndln* and *Lederhosen*, dancing some traditional mountain jig. These same people also perform at evening *Schuhplatter* sessions or whatever the local equivalent is.

All this, of course, belongs more to what we like to think of as a typical Alpine village — cuckoo clock houses nestling in a secluded valley surrounded by pine trees and usually requiring a major expedition to get to the slopes.

The ski-from-the-doorstep purpose-built space age resort does not go in much for this sort of thing. The nearest they get to it on their picture postcards is photos of the local marmots or reprints of the old mountain hut that used to be there before the bulldozers moved in.

Instead of having wizened old men on their postcards, these newer villages are more likely to feature personality pictures of the resort's rather famous 'Director'. Most of them have one — usually a ski teacher or architect who has lent his name to the project. You will usually have a chance of shaking hands with the *maestro*, if not actually being told to bend your knees by him, in the course of a week's stay.

Many resorts also have a local skiing hero who was born or lives nearby,

encouraging us to hope that some of his magic may rub off on us. He probably grew up in a remote mountain cabin and so had to learn to ski to get down to the village school or set the bear-traps up on the mountain.

The rest of the folk who staff the resort can be divided, for the sake of convenience, into two basic groups — those who are there to look after you and those who are there to push you around. It's a sort of Alpine adaptation of the nice/nasty principle used in interrogations.

The hard men are those out on the slopes, most notably the instructors, who order you about and put you through it even in appalling weather conditions. Even more objectionable are the people who run the ski-lifts — a universally surly breed — who always demand to see your lift pass at the most inconvenient moments, like when you're just about to grab hold of the T-bar. Their colleagues manning the cable cars where they pack people in like commuters on the Tokyo underground are equally unpleasant. Nor should one forget the ratrac drivers. You may never see their faces but they make no secret that their aim is to run you down at every available opportunity. The alternative name for their vehicle — *piste* bully — just about sums them up.

It's worth noting that gratuitous unpleasantness on the slopes is now more of a European speciality. The Americans have broken with this tradition and even have pleasant lift men who say 'Have a nice day' as you climb aboard. There are even 'ski hostesses' in some resorts to try to make you feel at home.

In the village, behaviour, in general, will be much more civilised. This is, after all, where they take your money and they have every reason to smile while doing it. The only likely exception is the ski hire shop. Here they seem to work on the theory that any trace of humanity on their part might encourage you to question whether the boots they are pushing are actually right for your feet; or whether it is normal to have poles coming up to your shoulders; or rust-caked bindings; or skis with big chunks carved out of the sole. But perhaps it's understandable. It's tough work forcing feet into boots that don't fit and overtightening bindings to ensure that people don't come back for readjustments (people don't normally bother to complain from the hospital). It must also be quite a strain calculating the enormous profits: a pair of skis hired out four times have already paid for themselves and then, as most of us know, they remain in service for ever. If it should occur to you to ask just how old your hire skis are, you will, of course, be told they were brand new at the start of the season.

The other emporiums will be rather more gracious to you. They appreciate the importance of the daily shopping ritual and try to make it as pleasant as possible. You could, after all, choose to spend the time between skiing and supper asleep in your hotel. And even if people do seem to spend an awful lot of time just looking, the shopkeepers know that before the week is out these browsers will have bought something from someone and that it may well be them. Unlike the hire business, they seem to have a certain sympathy for their victims. For there is no doubt that is what you are; if you need something on the mountain there's nowhere else you can go to get it. One word of warning, though; they can sometimes be a little mischievous with their advice, like persuading you that you really can't do without a bright yellow baseball cap or a fur-lined balaclava.

In the hotels and bars, too, people are capable of being quite pleasant – whether they make your *Lumumbas* and *Glühwein* or shake out your duvet of a morning. The most *gastfreundlich* are invariably the *patrons* of the individual establishments. Many of them are local characters and often have distinguishing features like bushy side whiskers. They enjoy their role as mine host and don't seem to mind if you have a good time.

15. Competition

'Who's going to come second?'

Harry Jerome, to the other sprinters on the starting line

One of the big attractions of skiing – for the Survival Skier at least – is that there is no score, and therefore no necessity to subject your abilities to possibly humiliating quantification. Anyway, there's no easy way to measure the skills of the Survival Skier. His art is so much more than can be summed up by the crude calibrations of a stop-watch over a slalom course. Championship skiing may produce a neat results table but it fails to take into account all the subtleties and complexities, the range of technique and resourcefulness that the Survival Skier must command to make his mark.

Nevertheless, it often takes the novice Survival Skier some time to realise that there is not much in racing for him; and there are some who never learn the lesson. When it comes to the Big Day the temptation of going home with a Golden Arrow or Platinum Chamois pinned to his anorak or some other useless ornament weighing down his suitcase proves too much. We all suffer from the delusion that we ski (or could ski) that much faster than the next man and it's all too easy to find ourselves signing up to try our luck between the sticks.

This temptation, or indeed compulsion, is most likely to affect those who have spent the week enrolled in ski-school. The class race on the final day is an established fixture and instructors usually insist that everyone takes part. However, if you really do want to opt out you can probably extricate yourself without difficulty by using standard Survival Skiing lines like:

'Never raced since I broke my leg in the Kandahar.'
'I'm trying to ski better, not faster.'
'Left my racing skis/boots at home this time.'
'My racing days are over now, I'm afraid.'

This type of remark is best pronounced with a sigh of regret, conveying that you did once have some racing days.

If you don't want to desert the field completely, you can offer to officiate – acting as a marshal, helping with the timing or just manning one of the gates. Thus you avoid active participation but remain involved as a sort of expert. There can be quite a lot of scope in this role. You wear your faded anorak with all the old badges on and, playing the veteran who knows all the heartaches, encourage, congratulate or console the competitors in your best avuncular manner.

Pleading safety first can be another way out. Shake your head, mutter something about the irresponsibility of the organisers, and say you don't fancy your chances in those ruts – not on compact skis anyway. It may not look it but that sort of snow can be absolutely fatal. You will always be vindicated as a number of people are bound to fall and some will hurt themselves. If you like, you can always wait for the first person to fall before pulling out.

There is, by the way, some truth in all of this. Statistics show that most skiing accidents take place on the penultimate day of a week's holiday — the day of the ski-school race.

Another perfectly sound tactic is simply not to be there when your name is called. There's always so much hanging about and delay anyway that it's not unusual for people to take off in frustration and mistime their return.

Alternatively, if you want to make a bit of a show, and pre-empt any accusations that you are chickening out, just ski the first three gates. By limiting yourself to just three gates it is usually possible to perform rather above yourself — skiing faster and more stylishly than you could ever hope to over the whole course. After three gates you then miss your turn and come out at the fourth, cursing angrily to yourself.

Many Survival Skiers, however, just will not take advantage of these sensible ways out. It's quite remarkable how many normally mild-mannered and well-balanced people become transformed into kamikaze competitors as soon as they tie a race number on. Something comes over them. The adrenalin starts to flow and they're set to do or die in an attempt to settle the arguments once and for all with their arch-rivals in the ski-class.

These confrontations, incidentally, never do settle the arguments. The results are never conclusive as at least one of the two is almost bound to make a mistake and fall or miss a gate. If they do both finish, the loser will argue that he was distracted by something, or lost his way, or that the course was harder (more rutted, icy, slushy) when he went down it.

So, for those who are determined to go through with it and who refuse to see reason on Race Day, here's some advice. If you want to win, make no attempt to ski properly. Any concession to style — attempting proper slalom turns, dipping the inside shoulder to shave the sticks — will be counter-productive. The only thing that counts is the time and the only way to get a fast one is to charge down. Forget about your sticks and carving your turns. Just concentrate on staying on your skis.

Some Survival Skiers have even developed a system which effectively amounts to *schussing* down. It depends, however, on the course not being terribly well set, which is often the case with a ski-school version of a giant slalom. The important thing is not to have to change direction too much. You have to be able to plot a more or less straight *schuss* line through several gates at a time. When you absolutely have to change direction you stop in a controlled crash. This is the hard part — you can't afford to waste too much time picking yourself up. Then you *schuss* off in the new line. Generally speaking, if more than two crashes are necessary, it's not worth your while.

Another alternative which requires the same sort of 'must win' desperation, or what the Americans would call PMA (Positive Mental Attitude), is the rollercoaster. It is important here to make sure you perform last. If you get called earlier you have to pretend to be adjusting your binding or something. Then just step into the deepest ruts made by the other skiers and let yourself go. You may break a leg; on the other hand if you stay on track you may win.

The other advantage of going last is that you may not even have to do the rollercoaster. It may well be that most of the others don't finish the course, particularly on an icy day, leaving you to ski sedately down to victory in a controlled and stately snow-plough.

One reason why so many people come to grief in the races is excessive preparation of their equipment the night before. They spend hours waxing and filing their skis and the next day they find them so unfamiliar that they have no control at all, particularly as they are trying to go super-fast. Some people are even silly enough to abandon their compacts for longer racing skis — a sure way of putting paid to their chances.

There's no reason, of course, why you shouldn't make your contribution to this de-stabilising process. While not normally recommending dirty tricks like sneaking into the ski-room at night and putting the wrong wax on your main rival's skis, there's no harm in being plenty generous with the old hip flask on the morning of the race. It's amazing how effective alcohol can be to *couper les jambes*. Ideally you should carry two or three hip flasks with different types of hard stuff in each, alternating the flasks at each tippling session.

Another way to bring disaster on your rivals is to tell them during practice runs — when they are probably skiing very close to their limits anyway — that they look as if they can go a lot faster still. They are then almost sure to go over the top in the race, spurred on, if necessary, by you shouting 'Go for it' and 'Hop, hop' at them. One of the surest ways of making someone fall is to go 'Hop, hop' at him.

There's always plenty of time to lubricate the joints and massage the ego of your opponents in this way as the race never starts on time. You are bound to spend at least two hours hanging around while the course is prepared, names are checked, numbers given out and the walkie-talkies set up properly. It's also more than likely that the other classes will have their races before yours.

On the whole, apart from softening up your opponents, it's best to have as little to do with this preparatory stage as possible. Otherwise the instructors will have you wasting an awful lot of energy fetching sticks, planting them and then snow-ploughing down the course to smooth it out.

Even when they start trying to group the classes together, calling everyone to

check in at the start, you can easily afford to stay clear a while longer. You can safely ski on down and catch the lift back up at least two or three more times before you're needed.

When it comes to the race itself, just do your thing and hope for the best. You can be sure the winning tactic will be either 'Who Dares Wins' or 'Slowly But Surely'. The problem is that you never know beforehand which it will be.

At the end of the day it never seems to matter all that much who won. At the presentation ceremony that evening everyone will get an impressive medal and certificate, at the very least, to take home. From some countries – Italy in particular – whether you finished the course or not you'll go back laden with magnificent medallions, elaborately inscribed scrolls and sporting statuettes that would make you the envy of many an Olympic champion.

For many people, though, the most prized memento will be the action photo taken as they nudged past the third gate, race number flapping in their slipstream, looking for all the world like an advertisement for racing skis. This is the reason why many competitors reject the 'do or die' approach – they want to make sure they are looking their best for the picture that will sit on the mantlepiece for some time, impressing the neighbours. So they take it very easily at the start, waiting to get into the camera sights at the third gate before going into their best racing crouch and composing the face into a look of rugged concentration.

The photographer, incidentally, will always be at the third gate; he can't afford to go too far down as a lot of competitors won't reach him. So even when you are using the early withdrawal ploy, it's always worthwhile waiting until the third gate before you pull out – if you want to be immortalised, that is.

After all, just because you didn't win there's no reason why you shouldn't look and feel as if you did.

That, anyway, is the principle that is likely to guide you and your fellow losers as you drown your sorrows. Afterwards it's usually not too hard to console yourself. And in the best Survival Skiing tradition, you can expect plenty of ego-restoring support from your comrades – provided you reciprocate. You should have no difficulty in agreeing, for instance, that hand-held timing, particularly with walkie-talkie communication, is no accurate way to determine the outcome of a big race any more.

Final Rules of Skiing

All skiers end the day with a tale to tell, if not several.

If you don't catch a cold on your holiday you will catch one immediately you return home.

It will all seem to have been much more fun when it's over.

The way you say it was is never quite the way it really was.

You will come again next year.
